SQUEAKING BY

U.S. Energy Policy Since the Embargo

SQUEAKING BY

U.S. Energy Policy Since the Embargo

RICHARD B. MANCKE

COLUMBIA UNIVERSITY PRESS
New York 1976

Library of Congress Cataloging in Publication Data

Mancke, Richard B   1943–
  Squeaking by: U.S. energy policy since the
embargo.

  Bibliography: p.
  Includes index.
  1. Energy policy—United States.   2. Power resources—United States.   3. Petroleum industry and
trade.   I. Title.
HD9502.U52M355   333.7   75-45438
ISBN 0-231-03989-1

Columbia University Press
New York   Guildford, Surrey

ACKNOWLEDGMENTS

Quotations from Leonard W. Weiss, "Antitrust in the Electric Power Industry," in *Promoting Competition in Regulated Markets,* edited by Almarin Phillips, copyright © 1975 by the Brookings Institution, Washington, D.C., appear with the permission of the Brookings Institution.

Tables 2.1–2.4 originally appeared in Richard B. Mancke, *Performance of the Federal Energy Office,* Washington, D.C.: American Enterprise Institute, 1975, and are reprinted with the permission of the American Enterprise Institute.

Table 7.7 originally appeared in Edward J. Mitchell, *U.S. Energy Policy: A Primer,* Washington, D.C.: American Enterprise Institute, 1974, and is reprinted with the permission of the American Enterprise Institute.

ACKNOWLEDGMENTS

CONTENTS

SQUEAKING BY
U.S. Energy Policy Since the Embargo

PART ONE

Failures of the U.S. Energy Policy

CHAPTER ONE

Preludes to the U.S. Energy Crisis

FULL-SCALE WARFARE erupted on Israel's Egyptian and Syrian borders on October 6, 1973. Seeking to aid their Arab brethren, members of the Organization of Arab Petroleum Exporting Countries (OAPEC) agreed to sharply reduce or, in the case of both the United States and the Netherlands, totally eliminate oil exports to all countries failing to adopt a pro-Arab foreign policy.[1] Because oil had no substitutes available at short notice, the shortages and higher prices triggered by the estimated 4.5-million-barrel cutback in OAPEC's daily oil exports threatened to precipitate worldwide economic havoc.[2] By January 1, 1974, the price of a barrel of crude oil at the Persian Gulf had tripled to about $8 and small quantities of crude were being sold on spot markets at prices in the neighborhood of $20.[3]

The United States suffered considerable economic damage as a result of the OAPEC embargo—primarily because its total energy costs soared to at least double pre-embargo levels.[4] However, even more important was the enormous damage to vital security interests. The near total inability of the United States and its European and Japanese allies to cope with the oil embargo reduced sharply the cohesion of the Western alliance; simultaneously, the embargo also led to the creation of a well-financed, politically savvy, and arguably hostile new world power—OPEC or any coalition of several major oil-exporting countries. The great success of the 1973–74 oil embargo raises the probability that a group of oil exporters will resort to this

This chapter makes extensive use of material that has appeared in Richard B. Mancke, "The Genesis of the U.S. Energy Crisis," in Joseph Szyiowicz and Bard O'Neill, eds., *The Energy Crisis and U.S. Foreign Policy* and in Richard B. Mancke, *The Failure of U.S. Energy Policy*.

tactic again in the future. Until this weapon is neutralized, vital security interests of the United States are endangered.

Why did the United States allow itself to become so vulnerable to the oil-embargo weapon? Many Americans have chosen to believe demagogic charges placing the blame on the selfish or incompetent actions of a variety of convenient scapegoats. Any litany of scapegoats must include:

1. the large monopolistic oil companies that reaped huge profits as a result of the worldwide oil shortage and therefore took steps to encourage it;
2. the Nixon Administration which failed to take any of the hard steps necessary to forestall this crisis and may have actually encouraged this crisis to help its "big oil" political allies; [5]
3. fuzzy-thinking environmentalists who made crisis inevitable by stubbornly thwarting most attempts to increase U.S. energy supplies;
4. and greedy consumers whose insatiable energy demands made shortages inevitable.

Each of these scapegoats had legitimate strong interests and involvements in energy matters. Hence, it was inevitable that each played key roles in molding several of the more important energy policy decisions made prior to the 1973–74 crisis. However, though these groups took steps to advance their own interests, they neither deliberately caused our energy problems nor deliberately precipitated the frequent failure of policies designed to remedy them. Instead, when viewed in toto, two other pernicious themes prevail: First, there was a widespread misperception of both the magnitude and, more important, the true nature of our energy problems; and secondly, those policies actually implemented were almost always too rigid and, frequently, were designed to achieve contradictory goals. [6] The search for scapegoats exaggerated both themes.

PRELUDES TO THE 1973–74 ENERGY CRISIS

Since the 1930s, every important U.S. energy policy has been aimed at achieving one or more of four desirable but sometimes contradictory goals:

1. Insuring the discovery and development of low-cost energy supplies adequate to meet our growing needs.

2. Preventing growing dependence on energy supplied from insecure (militarily or politically) sources.
3. Reducing the environmental pollution that is a by-product of most production, distribution, and consumption of energy.
4. Reducing the arbitrary transfers of billions of dollars from oil consumers to oil producers and owners of oil lands.[7]

Americans spent billions of dollars annually during the 1950s and 1960s attempting to achieve these worthy goals. Unfortunately, evidence of the type summarized below documents the failure of these attempts.

Too Much American Oil:
A Problem from the 1930s to the 1960s

Crude oil prices plummeted during the 1930s because the Depression led to a sharp fall in oil demands at the same time that the discovery and speedy development of the giant East Texas field led to a sudden surge in supply.[8] Prices fell so low that a few Texas producers allegedly found they could cut their losses by dumping "surplus" crude oil into nearby creeks. Faced with this "conservation" crisis, the major oil-producing states of the American mid-South (Texas, Louisiana, New Mexico, Oklahoma, and Kansas) adopted a policy—called market demand prorationing—designed to give each state control over the total supply of crude oil produced by firms doing business within it.

The mechanics of market demand prorationing were simple. First, the state set each well's maximum allowable daily production. The size of this so-called basic allowable production depended on two parameters: the well's depth and the number of acres it drained. Concern with cost rather than productivity provided the rationalization for the basic allowable formula. Specifically, because deep wells were more costly than shallow wells and total costs were higher when more wells were drilled on a tract, the states were persuaded that it would only be "fair" to give higher basic allowables to oil fields with deeper wells and/or densely drilled tracts.[9]

Promoting conservation provided the official rationale for prorationing. Nevertheless, the actions of the oil states' prorationing commissions suggest that conservation was not really their chief concern. Instead, they viewed as their principal assignment maintaining or raising crude oil prices by restricting available supplies. Because monthly oil demands fluctuated widely and producers could always raise their basic allowables by drilling more or deeper wells, successful performance of this assignment was not easy. In addition, problems arose because oil produced in any specified state faced competition from oil produced in other states. To solve these problems, two additional tools were necessary.

The problem caused by fluctuating demands and growing supplies was solved by refusing to let each well produce its basic allowable. Instead, each of the major prorationing states asked the largest buyers of their crude oil how much they expected to buy in the following month. With this information, any oil state could estimate quite accurately the monthly demand for its oil. The prorationing states then calculated the forthcoming month's "market demand factor" by dividing these estimates of the total demand for their oil by the total of all basic allowables. Finally, each prorated well's actual output during the next month was restricted to the product of its basic allowable and the state's market demand factor. Until the late 1960s, the supply restriction due to prorationing was severe. To illustrate, from 1960 through 1965 Texas wells were always restricted to producing less than 30 percent of their basic allowables.

Use of market demand prorationing gave several of the largest oil-producing states a precise instrument for controlling their producer's total outputs. However, failure to coordinate their prorationing policies could still result in interstate competition for higher oil sales and, hence, lower prices. In order to forestall this possibility, the major oil-producing states coordinated their prorationing activities through the office of the Interstate Oil Compact Commission. The U.S. government also provided some assistance.[10]

The oil states' enforcement of market demand prorationing did help to reduce the problems of overproduction plaguing the American oil industry during the 1930s. Unfortunately, the remedy ultimately proved far more costly than the illness it was designed to cure. The costs were of two kinds. First, since oil fields with deeper, more closely spaced wells were rewarded with higher basic allowables and since inefficient stripper wells (i.e., wells producing less than 10 barrels per day) were exempted from all output restrictions, prorationing created strong incentives for wasteful overdrilling. Second, by using prorationing, the large oil-producing states were able to restrict severely total crude oil output and, thereby, helped to keep prices for U.S. crude oil far above the competitive level until the late 1960s. The annual cost of prorationing to the U.S. economy was in the neighborhood of $2.5 billion in the early 1960s.[11] The days when the United States was burdened with "too much" oil are now a fading memory. Since 1973, most fields have been allowed to produce 100 percent of their basic allowables. Hence, enforcement of prorationing does not presently impose high costs on the U.S. economy.[12]

Consumers of American oil were the principal victims of market demand prorationing. The principal beneficiaries included:

1. Owners of oil lands who reaped sharply higher rents (royalties and lease bonuses) because prorationing raised the price at which they could sell any commercial oil found on their lands.
2. The oil-producing states that received higher rents from state-owned lands and also reaped higher severance taxes on all crude oil produced within the states.
3. Domestic producers who reaped windfall profits whenever prorationing was tightened so that they could sell their product at a higher price.[13]

The interests of these three groups have not always coincided. Indeed, disputes have sometimes raged between members of the same group. Nevertheless, because in many instances their interests have coincided, members of these three groups are frequently labeled as the domestic oil interests.

Running Out of Natural Gas

Natural gas was the United States' fastest growing major energy source between the close of World War II and 1970. Total U.S. energy demands more than doubled between 1945 and 1970. Over the same period, the share of total energy demands satisfied by natural gas rose from one-eighth to one-third. Unfortunately, U.S. production of natural gas had virtually stopped growing by the start of the 1970s. Even worse, it actually began to decline in 1972. The United States began to suffer an ever-worsening natural gas shortage. As a result, between 1970 and 1973 the annual rate of growth in U.S.

demand for crude oil products—natural gas's closest substitute— soared to 6 percent, nearly double its pre-1970 level. By 1974, the average daily excess of natural gas demand over supply was equivalent to around 3 million barrels of crude oil. Since U.S. production of crude oil also began to fall in the early 1970s, soaring oil imports proved to be the ultimate and very costly consequence of the ever-worsening natural gas shortage.

The present natural gas shortage is not due to nature's stinginess; it is man-made. Its proximate cause has been the Federal Power Commission's (FPC) enforcement of low ceiling prices on all interstate sales of natural gas. Because they have been too low, these price ceilings have discouraged firms from exploring for and developing new natural gas reserves.[14] What has been the justification for this pernicious policy?

The Natural Gas Act of 1938 authorized the FPC to regulate interstate pipelines in order to "protect consumers against exploitation at the hands of the natural gas [pipeline] companies." [15] This was thought to be necessary because of the "great economic power of the pipeline companies as compared with that of communities seeking natural gas." [16] Since a single interstate pipeline is typically the sole supplier of natural gas in most markets, protecting its consumers from possible monopoly exploitation is a valid policy goal.

The scope of the 1938 act was ambiguous. Until the early 1950s the FPC maintained that it was not empowered to regulate the prices pipelines paid gas producers; instead the Commission held that it could only regulate the prices charged for interstate pipeline services. As long as natural gas wellhead prices stayed near their Depression levels, there was no consumer opposition to the FPC's ruling. This consumer indifference evaporated quickly after the rapid expansion of interstate pipeline capacity led to huge postwar increases in natural gas demand. As demand increased, so did the wellhead price. Consumer representatives reacted to these higher prices by asking the FPC to reverse its decision not to control them. Two justifications were, and continue to be, offered. Most frequently heard (initially) was the justification that such price controls were necessary because natural gas producers were exploiting their monopoly power. In its 1954 Phillips decision, the Supreme Court implicitly accepted this justification and ruled that the Natural Gas Act did require the FPC to regulate wellhead prices.[17] Commenting on this justification, Professor Paul MacAvoy wrote:

> Regulation is generally conceded to be a doubtful propriety if the reasons for imposition of controls were fallacious. Regulation [of natural gas wellhead prices] was advocated in the courts and Congress to prevent monopoly prices in the Southwest. Studies of most field and supply markets in Texas, Louisiana, Oklahoma, etc., indicate the presence of systematic competition . . . throughout the period in which regulation was proposed. The problem to be solved by regulation seems not to have existed, so that the court mandate was given for "wrong" reasons. The necessity for Federal Power Commission regulation is doubtful.[18]

The second justification offered for FPC regulation of natural gas wellhead prices was that higher prices would not lead to appreciably higher outputs; rather, they would only lead to windfall profits for owners and producers of natural gas. Available evidence does not support the assumption that natural gas supplies are not price responsive.[19] This evidence has been conveniently ignored by those favoring natural gas wellhead price regulation. Instead, they have preferred to offer populistic arguments like the following: "Reduced to its simplest terms, the issue is whether Mr. Getty shall buy a yacht . . . or whether thousands of New Jersey commuters shall enjoy an extra evening 'on the town' in Manhattan once a year." [20]

The FPC's initial attempt to regulate wellhead prices proved unsuccessful. Natural gas wellhead prices nearly doubled between 1954 and 1959. Faced with this fact, the Supreme Court ruled in the CATCO case (1959) that the FPC's wellhead price regulation procedures were inadequate.[21] The FPC responded to the CATCO decision by adopting area-wide wellhead price regulation in September, 1960. This regulation proved effective. Natural gas wellhead prices hardly rose throughout the 1960s, even though demand continued its rapid growth. Initially, these price controls had no adverse consequences. However, by the late 1960s this was no longer true. Buyers of interruptible gas supplies were the first victims of natural gas shortages. They found their supplies terminated during winter. Since the late

1960s, another rationing device has been increasingly used: the blanket refusal to provide service for broad classes of potential consumers. Those unable to get natural gas service have suffered high costs. To illustrate, during the winter of 1974–75 it cost only one-third to one-half as much to heat the typical home with natural gas as with distillate fuel oil, its closest substitute.

To summarize, the FPC's enforcement of stringent wellhead price ceilings has led to a large, fast-growing shortage of natural gas. As time passes, and the shortage worsens, it becomes less likely that the monetary savings reaped by those fortunate consumers who can obtain all (or most) of the natural gas they desire at the low ceiling price offsets both (1) the larger monetary losses suffered by natural gas suppliers and consumers denied service and (2) the high costs suffered by the entire nation because worsening shortages of natural gas imply, as a corollary, increased reliance on insecure foreign oil and greater environmental pollution. Unfortunately, because Congress faces strong pressure from those consumers who benefit from "low" natural gas prices and because the myths persist that the supply of natural gas is price-inelastic and that its production is monopolized, legislation abolishing FPC wellhead price regulation of natural gas had not been passed as of late-1975.

Where Was That Alaskan Oil?

Atlantic-Richfield discovered the Prudhoe Bay oil field on the Alaskan North Slope in 1967.[22] Prudhoe Bay's 9.6-plus billion barrels of proved reserves make it the largest oil field known in North America. In 1969, Prudhoe Bay's owners decided that the cheapest way to deliver this oil would be to pipe it 900 miles across Alaska to Valdez, an ice-free but earthquake-prone port on the northeast shore of Prince William Sound on the Gulf of Alaska. At Valdez it would be loaded onto large tankers destined for the West Coast. Prudhoe Bay's producers planned to build a pipeline that would ultimately be able to pump 2 million barrels of crude oil daily and initially expected to start deliveries in late 1972. These expectations were not realized—primarily because a coalition of environmental groups obtained an injunction preventing the U.S. Interior Department from issuing the necessary pipeline construction permit until it had evaluated

the adverse environmental effects attributable to the pipeline and examined the environmental impact of alternative means of supplying
American consumers with similar quantities of energy. The Interior
Department did not complete its environmental impact statement until
the spring of 1972.[23] Opponents then challenged both the adequacy
of this review and the Interior Department's authority to grant a pipeline right-of-way of the necessary width. The Court was persuaded by
these arguments and continued to enforce its injunction. The issue
remained unresolved until late 1973 when Congress, following the
onset of the OAPEC embargo, passed special legislation allowing
construction of the Trans-Alaskan Pipeline (TAPS).[24] If the construction timetable is met, crude oil should begin flowing through TAPS
in mid-1977 at an initial daily rate of 1.2 million barrels.

Large shipments of Prudhoe Bay's crude oil would have been very
useful during the 1973–74 OAPEC embargo. Many chose to blame
environmentalists for its absence because of their opposition to
TAPS. Such criticism would be appropriate if the TAPS opponents
had adamantly opposed all plans to deliver Prudhoe Bay's oil; but
they did not. In fact, their intent was constructive. Specifically, they
pressed for two things: that the pipeline be built through Canada and
that additional environmental safeguards be required. Because of the
huge volumes of oil to be shipped from the North Slope and the
unusually rugged but ecologically fragile terrain this oil must traverse, both the Interior Department and the pipeline's developers
eventually acceded to the need for additional environmental safeguards. There were also three strong environmental reasons for pre-
ferring a trans-Canadian route:

1. TAPS would traverse earthquake-prone regions; the Canadian route
   was not as seismically active.
2. Oil shipped via TAPS must be transshipped via tankers to the West
   Coast; some oil spills are inevitable. The flow of oil through the Canadian pipeline would be uninterrupted between the North Slope and
   upper Midwest refineries.
3. Because of the large quantities of oil and gas known (or suspected) to
   be in northwestern Canada and the Alaskan North Slope, there were
   already plans to build both natural gas and crude oil pipelines across
   Canada to the United States. At the time of the Alaskan pipeline

debate, it seemed certain that one or both of these pipelines would be built during the 1980s regardless of whether TAPS was built. The damage to wildlife nesting patterns and migration flows, arctic permafrost, and virgin wilderness could be greatly reduced if all arctic pipelines traversed a common corridor. Since, at that time, it was believed that these other pipelines must go through Canada, these huge environmental savings appeared possible only if TAPS was not built. [25]

In addition to being environmentally preferable, the trans-Canadian route looked no worse than TAPS when judged by either economic or security-of-supply criteria. Admittedly, TAPS would be cheaper to build and could be constructed more quickly. However, these advantages were roughly offset by three factors:

1. Alaskan oil was more valuable (i.e., would command a higher price) in the Midwest than on the West Coast. [26]
2. Alaskan oil was less subject to military interdiction if shipped via an all-land route.
3. The choice of a Canadian route would have accelerated the rate of exploration and commercial development of suspected large oil and natural gas fields in the arctic regions surrounding Prudhoe Bay.

Construction of any trans-Canadian pipeline would require the support of the Canadian government. At the time of the Alaskan pipeline debate, Canada appeared to favor a trans-Canadian route because it would facilitate the development of its frontier oil and gas regions. But the United States never pursued this matter with the Canadians. United States–Canadian cooperation on energy matters began to deteriorate sharply following the OAPEC embargo when Canada imposed heavy taxes on crude oil exports and announced plans to gradually phase out all Canadian oil exports to the United States. Since Canada was the largest foreign source of secure oil supplies for the United States, any deterioration in the two countries' bilateral energy relations must hurt U.S. oil security. It seems probably that the deterioration of bilateral energy relations would not have been as sharp if, at the time of the embargo, their energy futures had been linked by a joint commitment to construct one or more trans-Canadian pipelines.

The unfortunate delays in delivering Alaskan oil illustrate a real problem. However, this problem was not obstructionism by environmentalists. They merely used the only tool available to try to persuade the U.S. government to impose more stringent environmental safeguards and to force it to seriously consider adoption of the seemingly preferable trans-Canadian route. Rather, the real problem was an inflexible administrative review procedure. On the one hand, the concerned administrators were unable to accept useful input from citizens having a legitimate interest in this matter. On the other hand, they were unable to prevent interminable delays before a ''final'' decision could be reached.

The Electricity Supply Crunch

Electricity brownouts became something of a tired running joke in the late 1960s. Brownouts occurred as a result of deliberate voltage reductions by electricity suppliers whenever there was a system overload; i.e., whenever electricity demands exceeded available supplies. Brownouts were occurring with increasing frequency because increases in electricity-generating capacity failed to keep pace with rapidly growing peak demands. This worsening shortage had several causes.

Electricity demand is highly cyclical: Hourly demands tend to be lowest in early morning and highest in late afternoon; daily demands tend to be highest at those times of the year that are either hottest, coldest, or darkest. Because it is prohibitively expensive to store large quantities of electricity, generating capacity used only for meeting peak demands is necessarily idle most of the time. For this reason, the extra unit costs of satisfying peak demands are relatively high: One study of a large New York utility concluded that the total cost of a kilowatt hour of electricity supplied to meet peak demands was more than twenty times higher than the cost of a kilowatt supplied during nonpeak periods.[27] With few exceptions, state public utility commissions have required electricity rates to be set so that peak and off-peak users pay the same unit price. Ignoring quantity discounts, this price is calculated by dividing the electric utility's total costs, including the return allowed to stockholders, by its total output. This type of average cost pricing effectively subsidizes high-cost peak consumption and this, in turn, encourages the rapid growth of peak-period demand.[28]

Rates that subsidize peak-period electricity consumption are undesirable. However, since public utility commissions have always enforced them, they cannot be blamed for the suddenly worsening electricity shortages since the mid-1960s. Shortages were largely due to three factors which, together, placed so many constraints on electric utilities that they found it increasingly difficult to construct new generating capacity. First, the public was becoming increasingly concerned about the environmental effects of the large quantities of waste products power plants discharged into the air and water and with the esthetic consequences of new power plants and transmission lines. Second, concern over the safety of nuclear power plants was mounting steadily. Third, new nuclear power plants did not perform as well as had been expected—maintenance problems led to unanticipated long shutdowns and many plants could not operate at their rated capacity.

Growing hostility to new power plants made it difficult to find acceptable sites.[29] This led to construction delays. Growing concern about power-plant wastes led to stronger pollution-control measures. Most important was the Clean Air Act of 1970. Stationary source emission standards implemented under the authority of this Act had the effect of discouraging construction of new coal-fired plants. Thus, electric utilities were forced to turn to plants fueled by low-sulphur oil or nuclear power. But low-sulphur oil was scarce and nuclear plants had not performed up to expectations and were under attack as unsafe. In sum, electric utilities suddenly faced a whole array of new constraints that had to be circumvented before they could increase electricity supplies. The motivations for imposing these constraints were desireable—they were the result of policies designed to alleviate what the citizenry correctly believed to be important problems. However, they did entail worsening electricity shortages and higher electrity costs.

Rising Dependence on Foreign Oil

Prior to the late 1940s the United States was self-sufficient in crude oil; the Gulf Coast states actually exported large quantities to Western Europe. However, by 1950, rapidly expanding exports from lower-cost Persian Gulf sources had nearly driven American oil out of European markets. Indeed, small but growing amounts of Persian Gulf oil were beginning to be sold in the United States. Rising oil imports could have only one consequence: undermining the oil states' previously successful efforts to fix a high price for American crude. Specifically, in the face of swelling imports, American crude oil's high price could be maintained only by continually tightening the oil states' prorationing policies. But, even if they succeeded in doing this, profits earned on domestic crude oil would be reduced because of a fall in its market share.

Owners and producers of domestic crude oil sought to prevent any significant erosion of their product's market share by persuading the federal government to restrict oil imports. Obviously, it would not be politic to confess selfish motives. Hence, they offered the following national security justification for oil import quotas: If the flow of oil imports was interrupted, the United States would face severe energy shortages until alternative supplies could be developed and/or steps could be taken to reduce demand. This could take several years. During the interim, the cost to the economy would be high because of the absence of short-run substitutes; even after the short-run shortage was over, costs could continue higher because the newly developed energy supplies would be more expensive than the oil previously imported.

Until the late 1960s the national-security justification for oil-import controls rang false. The United States imported relatively small quantities of oil and virtually all came from what were (pre-1970) militarily and politically secure Caribbean or Canadian sources. Prolonged interruptions from either source were unlikely. Moreover, even if they did occur, the United States had ample reserves of domestic supplies. Nevertheless, accepting the then false national security rationale in toto, President Eisenhower established mandatory oil import controls in 1959. In a decision that was to have major political ramifications, he decided that the valuable rights to import the limited amount of foreign oil permitted under the quotas should be allocated by giving them to refiners and (later) petrochemical producers.

Enforcement of import quotas encouraged domestic crude oil producers to raise outputs by restricting the price competition offered by foreign oil. More precisely, by restricting imports, the demand for domestic crude oil was effectively raised and this higher demand could be satisfied only by a rise in domestic output. The enhancement of national security attributable to this higher domestic output was the alleged benefit from an oil-import control policy. Its cost was the higher prices necessary to persuade domestic producers to raise their output. President Nixon's Cabinet Task Force on Oil Import Controls estimated that they cost American consumers roughly $4.8 billion in 1969.[30] A large part of these higher consumer costs represented higher incomes for the owners and producers of oil and higher tax revenues for the leading oil-producing states.

Arguments over the legitimacy of the high-income transfers resulting from the enforcement of oil-import quotas were inevitable. They were of two types. On the one hand, those living in regions of the United States producing little or no oil complained that the prices they paid for refined oil products were unfairly high; the beneficiaries from higher domestic oil prices strongly disagreed. On the other hand, recipients of the valuable rights to import cheaper foreign oil repeatedly offered reasons why each deserved a higher share. These two arguments were merged after what became known as the Machiasport controversy.

Because of their distance from the petroleum sources near the Gulf Coast, residents of New England have always paid relatively more than residents of other parts of the country for both refined oil products and natural gas. Also, not owning any oil lands, they do not receive any of the oil rents. As a results, the New England Congressional delegation consistently spearheaded the attack against oil-import quotas. In 1968 Occidental Petroleum proposed a plan that it claimed would reduce New England's heating-oil prices 10 percent: Occidental would build a 300,000-barrel-per-day refinery at Machiasport, Maine, if it were granted rights to import 100,000 barrels of crude oil daily. Under the 1969 quota-allocation formula, Occidental's proposed Machiasport refinery would have been allowed to import less than 30,000 barrels of crude oil daily. Since the right to import one barrel of oil was worth about $1.50 in 1969, acceptance of Occidental's request would have rewarded it with an additional daily subsidy worth in excess of $100,000. Since total oil imports were strictly limited by the quota, Occidental could have been rewarded more import rights only if other refineries were rewarded less. Thus, the entire additional subsidy requested by Occidental would have been at the expense of competing refiners.[31]

After Occidental made its Machiasport request the battle was joined: the New England Congressional delegation supported Occidental's proposal, the oil states and competing refiners were strongly opposed. In an effort to resolve this ticklish political problem, President Nixon established a prestigious Cabinet task force to undertake a comprehensive review of U.S. oil-import restrictions. Reporting to the President in 1970, the Oil Import Task Force concluded that the quota bore "no reasonable relation to current requirements for protection of either the national economy or of essential oil consumption." [32] To remedy this problem, the Task Force recommended that oil-import quotas be phased out and replaced with a high—but over time declining—tariff. After studying this recommendation for several months, the President rejected it. As his critics delighted in pointing out, this decision undoubtedly reflected political considerations. After all, the "oil lobby" could provide useful aid both to an incumbent President pursuing a "Southern Strategy" and to a likable Republican—George Bush—in the midst of a run for the Texas Senate seat. Also, abolishing the quota would reward Senators Edward Kennedy and Edmund Muskie, two leading contenders for the 1972 Democratic Presidential nomination. These political considerations must have been strong. However, President Nixon did have valid nonpolitical justifications for his decision. In particular, because of delays in obtaining Alaskan oil and the disappearance of "surplus" oil in the U.S. "lower 48" (i.e., states that share contiguous borders), it became apparent that domestic oil production would not reach the levels that the Oil Import Task Force predicted. Simultaneously there was a near doubling in the annual growth rate of U.S. oil demands because natural gas shortages necessitated higher demands for its closest substitute, distillate fuel oils; stationary source emission standards forced utilities to substitute residual fuel oil for coal, and motor vehicle emission standards resulted in reduced engine efficiencies and thus higher gasoline demands. For the reasons just cited, it was already becoming evident by mid-1970 that the Oil Import Task Force's projections of U.S. oil-import dependence were far too low and, therefore, that it had underestimated the possible damage to the United States from oil-import interruptions.

The battle over oil-import quotas continued to rage until they were abolished by a Presidential executive order issued in April 1973. In retrospect there can be no doubt that controls restricting U.S. oil imports were bad throughout the 1960s. They cost consumers billions annually and whatever security they provided was superfluous because, prior to the 1970s, the United States never faced a valid oil-security threat. However, by 1970–71 the situation had begun to change: U.S. dependence on oil imports was beginning to grow rapidly and there were no longer ample domestic reserves that could be brought on stream within a short time. Even worse, because of improved coordination among members of the Organization of Petroleum Exporting Countries (OPEC), sizable interruptions in the flow of oil imports became a real and growing possibility.

Upon its formation in 1960, OPEC's announced purpose was to prevent further falls in world oil prices. Throughout the 1960s the cartel failed to achieve this goal. However, at the Tehran Conference in January 1971, OPEC's prospects suddenly improved. After threatening to cut off all oil exports, OPEC succeeded in negotiating a 50-cents-per-barrel price rise. In return it agreed to guarantee stable and predictable oil prices for five years. This guarantee remained in force for about four months. Then OPEC reopened negotiations to demand more money. Subsequent repetitions of this blackmail scenario have made it chillingly familiar.

After OPEC's Tehran success, the United States faced a very real oil-security threat. Unfortunately, primarily because of the virulence of the oil-import quota debate, few American realized the possible dimensions of this threat prior to the onset of the OAPEC embargo in October, 1973. Hence, it proved politically inadvisable for the President to take any of the difficult steps necessary to alleviate an increasingly dangerous oil-import dependence. Indeed, responding to strong pressure from oil consumers and Senate critics from 1970 to 1973, he periodically relaxed the oil import quotas in order to prevent rises in domestic crude oil prices.[33] As a result, the United States' oil-import dependence soared at roughly a 30 percent annual rate during the early 1970s—leaving it ill prepared to deal with an oil embargo.

WHY U.S. ENERGY POLICIES FAILED

The five examples just discussed illustrate important instances when U.S. energy policy failed. These examples are by no means exhaustive.[34] Nevertheless, they suffice to illustrate that the twin themes of contradiction and misperception rather than deliberate malfeasance lie at the heart of past failures of U.S. energy policy. Rather than buttress this thesis with additional examples, it is probably more useful to search for general causes. There appear to be two: the inability or unwillingness to coordinate existing policies, and the failure to adopt flexible policies responsive to the ever-changing factual scenarios the United States faces.

Poor Policy Coordination

The energy policy of the United States emanates in bits and pieces from a variety of different power centers. On the eve of the OAPEC embargo, the most important included five Cabinet departments—Interior, Treasury, State, Defense, and Commerce, and four administrative agencies or regulatory commissions—Atomic Energy Commission, Cost of Living Council, Federal Power Commission, and the Environmental Protection Agency. Within many of these there were several competing sub-power centers and all were subject, in varying degrees, to input from a plethora of concerned congressional committees, presidential assistants, the Office of Management and Budget, courts, concerned industries, mineral landowners, state governments, and the general public. By deliberate design as much as mere neglect, each of these power centers saw only a part of our total energy problem and typically represented only a few of the legitimately concerned interests. Prior to the OAPEC embargo, all efforts to coordinate the policies of these different power centers failed.

Inflexible Policies and Ambiguous Facts

Besides fragmented policymaking, the other cause of the failure of the U.S. pre-embargo energy policy stemmed from its adoption of inflexible policies that could not be adjusted to take account of inevitable changes in the fundamental "facts" upon which they were based. At any time these facts are ambiguous because of the lack of hard data about such important parameters as the long-run price responsiveness of demand and supply for the major kinds of energy, the speed with which secure domestic energy supplies can be expanded, and the security of energy supplies from different foreign sources. The ambiguity of such facts is directly attributable to underlying geological, technological, and political uncertainty. It can only be alleviated as better knowledge gradually accumulates over time. As the costly failures of such policies as natural-gas wellhead price ceilings and mandatory oil-import controls illustrate, whenever there is considerable uncertainty about future conditions affecting a regulated industry, it is poor strategy to blindly ahdere to an inflexible policy whose success depends on the occurrence of a specific and frequently unlikely chain of events. Instead, a flexible groping strategy is advisable. Initially, a large variety of policy options should be pursued; more resources should, of course, be devoted to those initially judged most promising or least costly; as time passes and it becomes possible to evaluate how well the different policies have worked, the failures should be cut back and, at some point, eliminated; the successes should receive a growing share of the government's total resource commitment.

CHAPTER TWO

The Performance of the Federal Energy Office

ROUGHLY 17 PERCENT of U.S. oil supplies were coming from Arab sources in October 1973 when the OAPEC members announced they would embargo all oil exports to the United States until it modified the pro-Israeli tilt of its foreign policy. Because OAPEC oil had no substitutes available at short notice, the petroleum shortages resulting from this embargo threatened to precipitate economic havoc in the United States. Responding to this impending crisis, President Nixon issued an executive order establishing the Federal Energy Office (FEO).[1] FEO was instructed to initiate whatever policies were necessary to alleviate the ill effects of domestic oil shortages.

OAPEC officially ended its embargo of oil sales to the United States in mid-March, 1974. By mid-April U.S. petroleum supplies had been restored to adequate levels. The immediate crisis over, FEO was replaced by the congressionally chartered Federal Energy Administration in early May.[2]

The FEO enjoyed a glamorous, hyperactive six-month existence. This chapter offers a brief but comprehensive obituary evaluating FEO's effectiveness during its short lifetime. This obituary, however, deliberately departs from the customary eulogy in an effort to glean valuable lessons for dealing with any future sudden interruptions in the supply of a key productive resource. It concludes that, on balance, the measures taken by the FEO actually worsened the U.S. oil-supply problems.

The most important lesson that emerges from this probe of the un-

Most of the material in this chapter first appeared in Richard B. Mancke, *Performance of the Federal Energy Office*. Discussion with Edward J. Mitchell, director of the American Enterprise Institute's National Energy Project, and the comments and criticisms of three referees helped to clarify several issues addressed in this chapter.

derlying causes of the FEO's policy failures concerns planning. The oil shortages caused by the OAPEC embargo were severe enough that Americans somehow had to be persuaded to reduce their oil consumption. Even if the FEO had made no policy mistakes, cutbacks in oil consumption of the necessary magnitude would have been painful. Prior to the OAPEC embargo, the United States government had only the vaguest plans for dealing with such a contingency. Thus, both Congress and the White House panicked when it occurred. Good decision making is at best difficult in such a crisis atmosphere. It becomes nearly impossible when the organization responsible for making speedy decisions lacks adequate staff, administrative traditions, and a well-defined decision-making hierarchy, and is subject to political pressures from a plethora of interest groups. The blame for these deficiencies cannot be placed on the FEO. They were inherent in its situation as a newly established agency. It lies with Congress and, especially, the President for failing to make adequate preparations to deal with an oil embargo.

CLOSING THE U.S. OIL-SUPPLY GAP

The most important problem facing the Federal Energy Office when it came into being was the need to prevent the United States from running out of oil. Realizing that substitutes for the embargoed oil were not available, and not wishing to draw down inventories and bring on more stringent future shortages should the embargo persist, the FEO responded with a conservation program initially designed to persuade, and if necessary to force, Americans to reduce their daily oil consumption by the entire 2.8 million barrels of crude oil or refined product equivalents thought to come from OAPEC sources.[3] The FEO pursued a two-pronged strategy. First, facing the possibility that other measures to circumvent the shortage would fail, it began extensive spadework for a rationing program that would force Americans to reduce their oil consumption by whatever amount might, ultimately, be necessary. Throughout December 1973 and early January 1974 this facet of the FEO's operations received the most public attention. It unleashed a flood of newspaper and television "specials" detailing the difficulties commuters would suffer if rationing were imposed. Fortunately, the oil shortages were neither so prolonged nor so severe as to warrant rationing.

The second tactic employed by the FEO was to plead with consumers to accept some hardship voluntarily (e.g., lower temperatures in homes and offices and less pleasure driving) in order to reduce their petroleum demands. To put teeth into its pleas for voluntary conservation, the FEO persuaded Congress to force the states to return to daylight saving time and (much more important) to cut maximum motor-vehicle speeds.[4] It also relied on a mixed policy of persuasion and allocation regulations designed to result in sharp cutbacks in the quantities of oil products—especially gasoline—refiners could sell.

In late December, motorists in many urban areas began to endure hour-long waits to buy gasoline. Long lines at gas stations were to become the most visible and noxious symptom of the energy crisis in the United States.[5] The December gas lines were chiefly caused by panic buying. Many motorists began ''topping-out'' their tanks with purchases of $1 or less because they feared more severe future shortages. As the lines began to lengthen, other motorists decided they, too, had better get in line. The panic was on.

The gas-station lines were even longer and more widespread at the end of January and February 1974. By then the reason was no longer panic buying—most motorists had learned that repeated topping-out was a wasteful and incredibly time-consuming practice. Instead, largely because of strict allocation regulations promulgated by the FEO, gas stations throughout the country now really were running short of gasoline. Misguidedly severe FEO policies imposed this painful, costly, and largely unnecessary symptom.

Table 2.1 presents monthly data on year-to-year changes in U.S. stocks of crude oil and refined products. These data established that, on balance, the FEO's policies induced an overreaction to the OAPEC embargo. On the eve of the embargo (October 5, 1973), although U.S. stocks of crude oil and all refined products except gasoline were slightly lower than the year before and most petroleum products were in tight supply, no important sector of the economy was suffering from a severe shortage of petroleum products.[6] Because U.S. petroleum consumption during the embargo averaged

Table 2.1
Year-to-Year Changes in U.S. Stocks of Crude Oil and Refined Products
(millions of barrels; percentage change in parentheses)

Period	Crude Oil (1)	Gasoline (2)	Jet Fuels (3)	Kerosene (4)	Distillate Fuel Oils (5)	Residual Fuel Oils (6)	Total Crude Oil and Products [a] (7)
Oct. 6, 1972 to Oct. 5, 1973	-10.80 (-4.2)	1.28 (0.6)	-5.95 (-19.7)	-0.73 (-3.3)	-0.29 (-0.1)	-7.90 (-12.3)	-26.87 (-3.1)
Nov. 3, 1972 to Nov. 2, 1973	-10.96 (-4.3)	2.92 (1.4)	-4.38 (-15.2)	1.86 (8.8)	6.81 (3.5)	-6.89 (-11.0)	-13.67 (-1.5)
Dec. 8, 1972 to Dec. 7, 1973	0.64 (0.2)	-6.72 (-3.1)	0.60 (2.2)	4.80 (24.1)	29.89 (16.8)	-0.83 (-1.5)	28.91 (3.4)
Jan. 12, 1973 to Jan. 11, 1974	1.23 (0.5)	-9.78 (-4.5)	3.35 (12.7)	4.20 (24.0)	44.66 (29.9)	-2.88 (-5.2)	43.69 (5.5)
Feb. 2, 1973 to Feb. 1, 1974	-4.96 (-2.1)	-3.83 (-1.7)	3.39 (13.4)	4.41 (27.5)	50.64 (38.4)	-2.85 (-5.8)	52.64 (6.8)
Mar. 2, 1973 to Mar. 1, 1974	0.89 (0.4)	9.79 (4.5)	4.42 (17.8)	2.16 (14.2)	36.54 (31.5)	-1.15 (-2.5)	58.22 (7.8)
Mar. 30, 1973 to Mar. 29, 1974	2.97 (1.2)	14.54 (6.8)	5.17 (19.6)	-1.21 (-6.9)	21.58 (19.5)	-1.47 (-3.2)	47.06 (6.2)
Apr. 27, 1973 to Apr. 26, 1974	7.39 (3.0)	20.48 (10.0)	4.30 (15.8)	-2.80 (-15.4)	18.36 (16.6)	1.76 (3.8)	51.85 (6.8)

Source: Raw data are from the American Petroleum Institute's weekly reports on stocks of crude oil and refined products as reported in the *Oil and Gas Journal*, October 1973–May 1974.

[a] Includes aviation gas and unfinished oils, not shown separately.

roughly 10 percent less than the year before, the FEO would not have been taking unecessary risks if it had adopted measures that allocated petroleum products so that stocks always remained slightly below year-earlier levels.[7] Unfortunately, Table 2.1 shows that the FEO did not do this. Instead, by late April, when the embargo was lifted, stocks of every product except kerosene had registered significant improvement relative to the year before.

A rough quantitative estimate of the reduction in available petroleum supplies because higher stocks were accumulated may be calculated. American petroleum stocks totaled 848 million barrels at the onset of the OAPEC embargo—27 million barrels, or 3 percent, below the year-earlier level.[8] However, by late April total stocks of crude oil and refined products were up by nearly 7 percent, or about 52 million barrels, compared with a year earlier (see Table 2.1, column 7). This means that, precisely during the months of the OAPEC embargo, total U.S. petroleum inventories improved by about 80 million barrels when compared with the previous year. The reduction in U.S. oil imports attributable to the embargo (assuming that they would have continued at October, 1973, levels in its absence) was about 130 million barrels. However, because of the inventory buildup precipitated by the FEO's "successful" efforts to reduce the quantity of petroleum products available for sale, the effective shortfall suffered by American consumers was roughly 1.6 times that level—approximately 210 million barrels.

What might have happened if the FEO had forced refiners to produce and offer for sale an additional amount of gasoline equivalent to the 80 million barrel net buildup of crude-oil and refined-product inventories that its actual policies fostered? According to Table 2.2, available U.S. gasoline supplies would have averaged nearly 11 percent higher during January–April, 1974, when gasoline was in tightest supply, if the FEO had encouraged oil refiners to maximize gasoline supplies while holding inventories of all petroleum products at their year-earlier levels. This "no-risk" allocation strategy would have totally eliminated the gap between potential gasoline demand (estimated, assuming no embargo) and available supplies. In other words, the long lines at gas stations were not necessary.

Why did the FEO overreact to the OAPEC embargo? A key reason

Table 2.2
Average Daily Available Supply, Potential Supply, and Potential Demands of Gasoline in the United States, January–April 1974
(millions of barrels)

Month	Actual Available Supply [a]	Potential Available Supply [b]	Potential Demand Assuming No Embargo [c]	Excess of Potential Supply over Potential Demand
January	5.880	6.547	6.363	0.184
February	5.846	6.513	6.529	−0.016
March	6.178	6.845	6.633	0.212
April	6.484	7.151	7.027	0.124

Source: Compiled from the weekly refinery reports of the American Petroleum Institute as reported in the Oil and Gas Journal, January 1974–May 1974.

[a] Assumed to be equal to the sum of (1) average daily gasoline production by U.S. refiners, (2) average daily gasoline imports, and (3) the net reduction in gasoline inventories.

[b] Assumes that petroleum inventories were not built up relative to the preceding year during the embargo, and that, instead, refiners were forced to produce an additional 80 million barrels of gasoline which they made available for sale in January–April 1974.

[c] Assumes no shortages and prices remaining at pre-embargo levels. Calculated as equal to gasoline consumption in the corresponding month of 1973 plus 5 percent, the amount by which gasoline consumption in the first nine months of 1973 exceeded that in the corresponding period of 1972.

was its focus on the wrong variable—the anticipated reduction in U.S. oil imports—rather than on the level of U.S. petroleum stocks. This proved unwise for two reasons. First, during the embargo the daily level of U.S. petroleum imports averaged more than 1 million barrels higher than initially predicted, primarily because the international oil companies successfully undertook the massive task of redirecting the world oil trade. In order to circumvent OAPEC's announced intention to impose the brunt of the embargo on the Netherlands and the United States, these companies began shipping to this country large quantities of non-OAPEC oil that normally would have gone elsewhere.[9] Moreover, because U.S. oil companies offered higher prices for them, imports of refined products did not fall by the amount predicted. In fact, for the first time in recent memory, high prices even pulled some gasoline and kerosene from the Soviet Union to the United States.

In addition to overestimating the cut in U.S. oil imports, the FEO did not take into account the indirect oil savings stemming from the voluntary reduction in U.S. demands for two substitutes, coal and natural gas. For reasons to be elaborated shortly, substitution of the "saved" coal and natural gas led to reduced demands for both distillate and residual fuel oils. This in turn, stanched the drain on U.S. petroleum stocks.

ALLOCATION PROBLEMS

The Federal Energy Office correctly realized that the American public would embrace its voluntary conservation measures only if its allocation of the costs of the oil crisis were demonstrably fair. Hence, besides making sure that the United States did not run out of oil, the FEO's major duty was to develop and implement policies to spread the burdens of petroleum shortages in an efficient and equitable way.[10] Seeking to do this, the FEO introduced allocation measures designed to place a heavier burden on users thought to be better able to reduce their consumption without severe economic disruption (for example, most industries except petrochemicals, trucking, and farming) or in some vague ethical sense less deserving (for example, motorists).[11] Unfortunately, even ignoring the complaints from each group that believed its share of the burden was unconscionably high, the FEO soon found that just and efficient allocation was no easy task. Four of its allocation problems are discussed below.

Allocation Between Gasoline and Distillate Fuel Oil

Gasoline and distillate fuel oils are quantitatively the two most important refined-oil products. Most gasoline is used to power motor vehicles; most distillates are consumed either in industrial and home heating or in fueling diesel engines. U.S. gasoline consumption averaged 6.6 million barrels per day in 1973; consumption of distillates averaged 3.2 million barrels.

Because, during winter, adequate home heating is obviously more

important to human life than most automobile travel, the FEO concluded that Americans would find it less disruptive if they reduced
their consumption of gasoline proportionately more than their consumption of distillate fuel oils. Hence, it repeatedly exhorted refiners
to produce more distillate oils and less gasoline. Besides exhortation,
it employed the price-setting powers delegated to it by the Cost of
Living Council to skew allowable refined-product prices so that distillate sales were more profitable than gasoline sales. Table 2.1 confirms that by early December 1973 stocks of distillate fuel oils far exceeded year-earlier levels. But simultaneously, those notorious
gasoline lines began to form. The FEO had overestimated the shortage of distillate fuel oil but underestimated the shortage of gasoline.
Even so, until late January 1974, the FEO continued to urge refiners
to produce more distillates at the expense of gasoline, and until mid-
February it manipulated refined-product price ceilings to achieve this
end. The burgeoning distillate inventories—they had soared to more
than 38 percent above year-earlier levels by early February—spurred
by this policy are plainly illustrated in Table 2.1. If the FEO had instead adopted policies that required refiners to maintain distillate
stocks at corresponding year-earlier levels, daily U.S. gasoline production could have averaged roughly 400,000 barrels (or 6.5 percent)
higher during the first four months of the OAPEC embargo (see Table
2.3).

Three factors explain why the FEO's emphasis on distillate fuel
oils proved to be misplaced. First was a fortuitous warm winter in the
more populous eastern half of the country. Second, in our car-depen-
dent society, most motorists were unwilling to make the significant
changes in life style that would have brought about immediate reductions in car miles traveled until they were forced to do so by "gas-
less" Sundays, alternate-day rationing, and the impossibility of finding fuel. Even when they were willing, changing long-ingrained
driving habits that resulted in high gas consumption required constant
vigilance. In contrast, significant reductions in demands for distillate
fuel oils followed directly from some extremely simple moves. Most
obvious, in northern climes use of fuel oil for heating could be cut
back 6 to 10 percent merely by turning down thermostats 6 degrees.
Third, because Americans voluntarily reduced their demands for coal

Table 2.3
Average Daily U.S. Production of Gasoline,
Actual and Possible, October 1973
Through January 1974
(millions of barrels)

Month	Actual [a]	Possible [b]	Excess of Possible over Actual (percent)
October	6.551	6.794	3.7
November	6.395	7.055	10.3
December	6.080	6.502	6.9
January	5.883	6.168	4.8
Four-month average	6.227	6.630	6.5

Source: Compiled from the American Petroleum Institute's weekly refinery reports as reported in the Oil and Gas Journal, October 1973–February 1974.

[a] Given FEO policies.

[b] Calculated by assuming that without the special encouragement that distillate production received from FEO policies, U.S. refiners would have produced sufficient amounts of distillate fuel oils to maintain stocks at corresponding year-earlier levels, and that any crude oil made available as a result of this decision was refined into gasoline.

and natural gas (which together supplied roughly 50 percent of total U.S. energy needs) by about 10 percent below predicted nonembargo levels, some industrial customers who normally used distillate fuel oil could turn to these other fuels. To illustrate, because U.S. supplies of natural gas were inadequate to satisfy winter heating demands, many industrial, commercial, and institutional users who bought natural gas on interruptible contracts expected their supplies to be stopped during winter. When this happened most would not shut down but, instead, would begin burning substitute fuels, usually propane or distillate and residual fuel oils. The voluntary cutbacks by natural gas users during winter 1973–74 reduced the number and duration of natural gas interruptions, thus lightening demands for distillate fuels. Because most automobiles must be powered by gasoline, no comparable reduction was experienced in gasoline demand.

Interregional Allocation of Gasoline

Some sections of the United States are much more dependent on oil imports than others. On the eve of the OAPEC embargo, well

over half of the Northeast's oil demands were being supplied from
foreign sources other than Canada. In stark contrast, the Gulf Coast
states had access to domestic supplies sufficient to meet all of their
needs. Obviously, after the onset of the embargo, considerations of
both efficiency and equity provided compelling reasons for allocating
large quantities of oil from relatively oil-rich to relatively oil-poor
regions.

Gasoline was the petroleum product in tightest supply throughout
the OAPEC embargo. In order to ensure that the available supplies
would be distributed equitably around the country, the FEO issued
regulations requiring that, after meeting certain priority needs (trucking and farming, for example), oil companies had to allocate gasoline
among their dealers according to sales in the corresponding month of
1972.

The FEO regulations did not achieve an equitable interstate distribution of gasoline supplies. As Table 2.4 shows, in February,
when gasoline shortages were most severe, initial allocations for the

Table 2.4
February 1974 Gasoline Allocations, by State
(millions of gallons)

State	Projected February Need	Initial February Supply	Supply as Percent of Need	Emergency February Allocation	Initial plus Emergency Allocation as Percent of Need
Wyoming	17.6	21.5	122	—	—
Louisiana	141.3	154.0	109	—	—
Kansas	99.0	106.9	108	—	—
Minnesota	159.9	164.7	103	—	—
Oklahoma	118.9	121.3	102	—	—
Texas	548.2	542.7	99	—	—
Hawaii	22.3	21.4	96	—	—
Arkansas	86.2	82.8	96	—	—
New Mexico	48.9	46.5	95	—	—
Colorado	105.4	99.1	94	—	—
Alaska	8.8	8.3	94	—	—
North Dakota	25.1	23.3	93	—	—
Idaho	32.5	29.9	92	—	—
Maine	37.5	34.1	91	3.4	100

State	Projected February Need	Initial February Supply	Supply as Percent of Need	Emergency February Allocation	Initial plus Emergency Allocation as Percent of Need
Washington	123.1	112.0	91	—	—
Nebraska	66.8	59.5	91	—	—
Delaware	22.8	20.3	89	2.0	98
D.C.	18.7	16.6	89	1.7	98
Massachusetts	184.9	162.2	88	16.2	97
New York	465.1	409.3	88	40.9	97
Michigan	343.4	295.3	86	—	—
Utah	44.7	38.0	85	—	—
California	791.4	672.7	85	—	—
South Dakota	31.0	26.4	85	—	—
Ohio	397.9	319.1	84	—	—
Tennessee	176.2	148.0	84	14.8	92
Wisconsin	162.9	135.2	83	—	—
Montana	33.0	27.4	83	—	—
Kentucky	126.2	103.5	82	10.4	90
Rhode Island	35.7	29.3	82	1.9	87
Florida	362.0	293.2	81	17.6	86
Iowa	123.5	100.0	81	—	—
Mississippi	97.2	78.7	81	7.9	89
South Carolina	112.1	90.8	81	9.0	89
North Carolina	214.9	171.9	80	17.2	88
Indiana	210.6	166.4	79	16.6	87
Missouri	199.0	155.2	78	15.5	86
Connecticut	112.4	87.7	78	8.8	86
Illinois	407.3	313.6	77	31.4	85
Pennsylvania	401.7	305.3	76	30.5	84
Maryland	146.8	110.1	75	11.0	82
Oregon	91.5	67.7	74	6.8	81
Alabama	143.4	104.7	73	10.5	80
Arizona	101.5	73.1	72	7.3	79
Georgia	242.9	174.9	72	—	—
Nevada	27.4	19.2	70	1.9	77
New Jersey	307.8	212.4	69	21.2	76
Vermont	19.6	13.5	69	1.4	76
West Virginia	58.6	39.3	67	3.9	74
New Hampshire	31.1	19.6	63	2.0	69
Virginia	233.0	146.8	63	14.7	69

Source: National Journal Reports, March 9, 1974. From data used by the Federal Energy Office.

states ranged from a low of 63 percent of projected needs in both New Hampshire and Virginia to a high of 122 percent of projected needs in Wyoming. States that produced large quantities of crude oil or bordered oil-exporting western Canada had the most gasoline— most of their residents suffered no direct discomfort from the OAPEC embargo. Hardest hit were five Eastern states whose initial allocations averaged only 66 percent of their projected needs. Obviously, in these and similarly situated states, stringent belt-tightening was necessary to reduce gasoline consumption to the low level of available supplies. And even that was not enough; large areas of most of these states ran out of gasoline at the end of both January and February.

Differential dependence on imported oil and transportation bottlenecks were the chief causes of the large interstate differences in gasoline supply. The existing network of petroleum-product pipelines did not have sufficient extra capacity to ship the necessary quantities of gasoline from relatively gasoline-rich to relatively gasoline-poor regions of the United States. Apart from this physical limitation, the allocation regulations helped to exaggerate interregional gasoline supply differences in three ways:

1. Basing allocation on 1972 sales hurt fast-growing regions disproportionately.[12]

2. In 1972 several major oil companies (e.g., British Petroleum, Gulf, Phillips) began consolidating retailing operations by closing several thousand stations in regions of the country where inadequate or obsolete refining capacity made retailing relatively less profitable. Normally these oil companies might have been expected to replace obsolete refining capacity with new refineries able to supply these markets at lower cost. However, because oil-import quotas were still in effect, builders of new refineries had no guarantee that they would be able to secure the necessary supplies of crude oil. Hence, prudence dictated that no new refineries be built.[13] Abandonment of gas stations was especially prevalent in the Southeast and Midwest. Since each oil company's available gasoline was to be allocated on the basis of its dealers' 1972 sales, these areas suffered a disproportionate fall in gasoline supplies.[14]

3. Like states, oil companies relied on imported oil in widely varying degree. Domestic crude-oil supplies of companies like Exxon, Getty, Gulf, and Marathon were sufficient to supply most of

their refineries' needs. In contrast, the embargo led to proportionately larger falls in output by crude-short refiners such as Ashland and Sohio. Those states, chiefly on the East Coast, with heavy concentrations of stations supplied by crude-short refineries suffered disproportionate gasoline shortages.

In addition to failing to correct the sharp inequities among states, the FEO's policies also led to misallocation of gasoline supplies within states. The long lines that were commonplace in most major Eastern urban centers from late December 1973 through February 1974 were unknown in many rural and vacation areas located in the same states. Urban areas suffered most because throughout the embargo drivers tended to fill their tanks close to home or work. The sharp reductions in pleasure driving and weekend trips meant that far fewer fill-ups took place in outlying rural and vacation areas.

Despite the good intentions of the FEO's program to allocate available gasoline supplies equitably among regions, it failed. Enormous interregional differences in gasoline supplies persisted throughout the embargo. A better policy would have allowed oil companies to charge slightly higher prices on sales to dealers in areas classified by the FEO as gasoline-short. Since the FEO's price controls on petroleum products did take account of interregional differences in gasoline production and delivery costs, allowing oil refineries to impose a surcharge of about 1 cent per gallon on sales in gasoline-short areas should have provided ample incentive for the elimination of the costly regional shortages.

Intertemporal Allocation of Gasoline

One of the most frustrating problems during the OAPEC embargo was the sharp worsening of gasoline shortages near the end of the month. These resulted in wasteful end-of-the-month transportation bottlenecks throughout the country. Paradoxically, these cyclical shortages arose largely from one of the FEO's pricing regulations: the decision to allow refiners and dealers to raise prices to offset higher costs only at the start of each month. Since crude-oil costs were soaring, this rule gave refiners a strong incentive to withhold gasoline at the end of a month for sale at the beginning of the new month, when they could charge a higher price.[15]

The gasoline shortages were especially severe at the end of February, when many Eastern motorists found it impossible to purchase gasoline. The blame rests squarely on the FEO announcement in mid-February that gas stations would be allowed to raise their profit margins from 8 to 10 cents on each gallon sold after March 1. A dealer's profit-maximizing response to this regulation change would be to lock up his station until March. Many did just that.[16]

The American motorists' monthly cycle of relative feast followed by absolute famine could have been largely eliminated by allowing refiners to pass through higher costs as they occurred and by allowing dealers to raise their profit margins on the date when rule changes were announced.

Interrefinery Allocation of Crude Oil

There are large differences in the degree to which American oil companies refine OAPEC crude oil. Those that were most dependent on OAPEC crude oil at the embargo's onset faced the severest shortages. They persuaded Congress that this situation was not equitable. As a result, Congress instructed the Federal Energy Office to establish a program requiring relatively crude-rich refiners to share supplies with their less fortunate competitors. To implement this directive, the FEO (as of February 1, 1974) ordered refiners with crude-oil supplies that exceeded the industry average to sell some of their "surplus" to crude-poor competitors. The maximum price a refiner could charge for its "surplus" was set equal to the weighted average of its total crude-oil costs from all sources. Because most price-controlled domestic crude oil cost several dollars less per barrel than foreign crude, crude-poor refiners like Ashland and Sohio found that they could reduce their costs by curtailing their own imports of non-OAPEC oil at $10-plus per barrel and, instead, buying "surplus" from crude-rich refiners like Exxon and Gulf for about $7. For the same reason, crude-rich refiners realized they would lose several dollars on every barrel of oil imported at $10-plus but sold at the lower average price. This regulation thus had the perverse effect of encouraging both crude-short and crude-rich refiners to cut back their oil imports during precisely those months when the OAPEC embargo was most effective.

To soften the impact on crude-rich refiners who were forced to sell crude oil to others, the FEO issued three supplemental regulations. First, the "84-cent provision" allowed crude-rich refiners to raise their refined product prices enough to capture an additional 84 cents of revenue for each barrel of crude oil that they were forced to sell. Second, they could add a 6 percent selling fee to their average crude-oil costs before making any sales to their crude-short competitors. Third, they could raise their prices for petroleum products by an amount equal to the reduction in their profits caused by the forced sale.[17] Taken together, these three supplementary regulations allowed crude-rich refiners to more than recover their total "losses" (that is, their potential but unrealized profits) due to forced sales. As a result, imports did not decline appreciably because of the FEO's inter-refinery allocation regulations.[18] In September 1974, John Sawhill, then head of FEO's successor, the Federal Energy Administration, accused the crude-rich refiners that took advantage of all three supplementary regulations of "double-dipping" because they recovered more than 100 percent of the reduction in their profits due to the forced sales of their crude oil and in the process overcharged consumers by $100 to $300 million.[19] Administrator Sawhill's criticism was too strong. First, the FEO staff apparently became aware of the possibility of double-dipping only when top officials of several major oil companies told them about it.[20] Second, many oil companies refrained from exercising their legal right to double-dip. A subsequent estimate of the overcharge was $40 million.[21] Third, the possibility of double-dipping arose only because the FEO established a cumbersome, poorly designed interrefinery allocation program that required complicated special exemptions to forestall severe disincentives to import oil.

Who Was Responsible for the Allocation Failures?

The policies of the Federal Energy Office did not achieve a just and efficient allocation of petroleum supplies among products, regions, refiners, or time periods. Many have charged the oil companies with the responsibility for these failures. After all, if the oil companies had not reached greedily for higher profits, the observed misallocation of petroleum supplies need not have been so severe. As the foregoing discussion amply documents, however, if the oil companies were at fault, it was because they responded in accordance with the price controls, the regulatory constraints, and the repeated public pleas of the FEO. Indeed, they would have deserved the strongest public censure if they had done otherwise during a period of national economic crisis.

At least some of the responsibility for the FEO's misguided allocation measures rests with the Congress whose Emergency Petroleum Allocation Act called for implementation of a comprehensive allocation program within thirty days of its passage. Though passed in November 1973, shortly after the OAPEC embargo was imposed, this act had been drafted six months earlier. At that time Congress was attempting to alleviate two other problems: (1) inadequate supplies of crude oil for independent refiners, who bought most of their crude-oil inputs, and (2) inadequate supplies of petroleum products for independent dealers, who since early 1973 had been cut off by refiners suffering from shortages of refinery capacity. In order to satisfy the intent of Congress to aid the independent dealers and its instructions to base allocations on what Congress regarded as more normal 1972 demand and supply conditions, the FEO geared its gasoline allocation measures to maintaining or reestablishing customer-supplier relationships that held in that year. Unfortunately, these had changed considerably by early 1974 because in the interval many independents, unable to get adequate gasoline supplies, had lost sales, acquired new suppliers, or left the business. Given the haste with which the FEO was created, its staff lacked both the size and the expertise to implement the complex and highly detailed measures necessary for adjusting the regulations to deal with these changes. Many of these administrative problems persisted until April 1974, when the embargo was over. If Congress had given the FEO greater administrative flexibility, many could have been avoided and the allocation measures might have proven more successful.[22]

PRICE CONTROLS

It was popularly believed that the large oil companies had helped to engineer the petroleum shortages during the OAPEC embargo in order to reap sharply higher prices and profits. No evidence has ever been presented to substantiate this belief. Nevertheless, the mere fact that so many Americans held it meant that their cooperation with the FEO's voluntary conservation measures depended on confidence in FEO's efforts to prevent profiteering from the shortage. The FEO used price-setting powers delegated to it by the Cost of Living Council in this effort. They failed. Understanding how and why requires some background.

Multi-tiered Prices for U.S. Crude Oil

Domestic crude oil prices were rising in early 1973. As part of its program to combat inflation and to prevent owners and producers of previously developed supplies from reaping windfall profits, the Cost of Living Council set ceiling prices on all crude oil classified as "old"—oil from leaseholds producing prior to 1973. The council believed that this action would not lead to reduced production of old oil because the out-of-pocket costs of exploiting most developed sources were far lower than the ceiling price. However, responding to pressure from politically powerful independent producers, Congress explicitly exempted from price controls the oil from low-productivity stripper wells that produced less than 10 barrels of crude oil per day.[23] Stripper oil production costs were already near the May ceiling price and rising sharply due to the rapid price inflation of drilling equipment and supplies. Hence, the justification for the stripper oil exemption ran, imposition of effective price ceilings would perversely discourage output, precisely at a time of tight supply, by making it unprofitable to continue producing from marginal fields, to rework closed fields, and to make the investment necessary for boosting output from stripper wells already in operation.

The Cost of Living Council also recognized that higher crude-oil prices would encourage oil companies to expand greatly their investments for exploration and for developing and producing oil from new sources. Hence, "new" crude—production from a leasehold above the level achieved in 1972—was also exempted from the price ceilings. To reinforce these incentives for the new exploration and development, a barrel of "released" crude was also exempted from the price ceilings each time a barrel of new crude was produced. During 1974 approximately 35–40 percent of all U.S.-produced crude oil was exempt from price controls (see Table 2.5).

Before the imposition of price controls, the price paid by oil re-

Table 2.5
Crude Wellhead Prices and the Percentage of Domestic
Production Sold at Controlled and Uncontrolled Prices

1974	Stripper Wells %	price	Uncontrolled New Oil %	price	Released Oil %	price	Controlled Old Oil %	price
Jan.	13	$ 9.82	17	$ 9.82	10	$ 9.82	60	$5.25
Feb.	13	$ 9.87	15	$ 9.87	10	$ 9.87	62	$5.25
Mar.	13	$ 9.88	16	$ 9.88	11	$ 9.88	60	$5.25
Apr.	13	$ 9.88	16	$ 9.88	10	$ 9.88	62	$5.25
May	13	$ 9.88	15	$ 9.88	10	$ 9.88	62	$5.25
June	13	$ 9.95	15	$ 9.95	10˙	$ 9.88	63	$5.25
July	13	$ 9.95	15	$ 9.95	9	$ 9.95	64	$5.25
Aug.	12	$ 9.98	14	$ 9.98	8	$ 9.98	66	$5.25
Sept.	12	$10.10	13	$10.10	8	$10.10	67	$5.25
Oct.	12	$10.74	14	$10.74	8	$10.74	66	.$5.25

Source: Federal Energy Administration, *Monthly Energy Review*, February, 1975.

finers for any specified barrel of crude oil corresponded directly with its economic value. Thus, premiums were typically paid for (1) higher-gravity crudes because they yielded proportionately more gasoline, (2) low-sulphur crudes because they were cheaper to refine and their products contained fewer pollutants and therefore were more valuable, and (3) crudes located relatively close to major refining and consuming centers. After the imposition of price controls, the price paid for a barrel of crude oil delivered to any specified American refinery also depended on whether it was classified as old, exempt (that is, new, released, or stripper oil), foreign, or some combination of the three. Table 2.5 shows that old oil was cheapest. Its average wellhead price was fixed at $5.25 per barrel throughout 1974. In sharp contrast, exempt oil of similar quality sold for nearly $10, and most foreign oil delivered to U.S. refineries in early 1974 ranged between $10 and $15 per barrel.[24]

Well before the start of the OAPEC embargo, it was evident that the price ceilings on old oil had been set far below market clearing levels, and, therefore, shortages had developed. Crude-short refiners, desperate for refinery feedstocks, bid up the price of exempt crude oil. Desiring even more oil, they began seeking ways to circumvent the price controls on old oil. According to reports appearing in the trade press prior to the OAPEC embargo, some succeeded by agreeing to tie together purchases of old and new oil from a given supplier: they bought old oil at the controlled price, but bought new oil at a price so high that the weighted average price for the total purchase rose to near the market clearing level.[25] Thus, the price controls on old oil had the undesirable consequence of accelerating the inflation of new oil prices.

U.S. petroleum supplies became much tighter after the OAPEC embargo. Realizing that producers of old oil would almost certainly require tie-in purchases in order to circumvent the price controls, the FEO froze all buyer-seller arrangements on old oil as of December 1, 1973. This ruling eliminated the possibility of tie-in sales and thereby saved the controls on crude oil prices from total ineffectiveness.

Some refiners process much greater proportions of old crude than others. In order to prevent these fortunate refiners from reaping vast windfall profits, the FEO had to enforce differential ceilings on the prices refiners could charge for their products. The method was to allow each refiner a specified markup over its full unit production costs. Application of the FEO's pricing rules resulted in intercompany differences of as much as 12 cents per gallon in retail gasoline prices.

All petroleum products were in short supply during the OAPEC embargo. Hence, even companies whose products carried prices as much as 12 cents per gallon higher than their competitors (because they processed proportionately more of the high-priced exempt and foreign crude) did not lose sales. However, once the embargo ended and the shortages eased, these companies would confront the dilemma of either maintaining their higher prices and watching their sales plummet or cutting prices and incurring huge losses. This situation was neither "fair" nor economically desirable. However, given multi-tiered pricing for crude oil, the unhappy choice could be avoided only by requiring relatively crude-rich refiners to sell to their competitors some of their cheap crude at controlled prices. Disregarding the vigorous protests of the crude-rich refiners, who felt, justifiably, that they were being asked to subsidize their less fortunate (or less astute) competitors, the FEO and its successor, the Federal Energy Administration, enforced the interrefinery allocation rules discussed earlier.[26]

The Failure of Crude-Oil Price Controls

The foregoing discussion provides a taste of the complexities of the price regulations of crude oil and of the problems arising from their enforcement. The Federal Energy Office was aware of most of these problems. It used much of its scarce manpower trying to make the controls more efficient and equitable and to enforce them properly, but to no avail. Unfortunately, because crude oil was in such short supply, inequities and inefficiencies were inherent in any system of effective price controls.[27] Perhaps even worse than the myriad problems that the controls caused was their failure to achieve one of their main goals, restraint on oil-company profits.[28] To illustrate, in the first quarter of 1974, in the aftermath of the OAPEC decision to embargo oil sales, earnings of thirty of the largest U.S.-based oil companies soared 78.4 percent over the same period in 1973.[29]

The FEO never questioned the desirability of preventing oil companies from reaping windfall profits due to the OAPEC embargo. In view of the need for voluntary public support for its energy-conservation plans and the enormous public distrust of the oil industry, this was a reasonable decision. But controlling windfall profits is not without problems. Most important, it places the government in the difficult position of defining acceptable profit levels. Judged by the most common measure—the rate of return on equity investment— profits of most U.S. oil companies were below the average for all U.S. industry for the ten years prior to the OAPEC embargo.[30] Largely as a result of the embargo, profits of 28 large oil companies rose 53 percent in 1973 and an additional 41 percent in 1974.[31] Their rate of return on equity reached 17.4 percent in 1974 compared to roughly 14.5 percent for all U.S. manufacturing.[32] These comparisons establish that 1974 was an unusually good year for the American oil industry. However, oil industry profits began falling in the last quarter of 1974. This trend accelerated during the first three quarters of 1975. Unusually high profits that last only one year are not sufficient to establish the contention that an industry's profits are "excessive" and should therefore be controlled.[33]

The price controls failed to check the rise in the oil companies' post-embargo profits for three reasons. First, the sharp rise in the price of foreign oil doubled the value of inventories of foreign crude oil. Large inventory profits were realized when crude bought at pre-embargo world prices was sold at post-embargo prices. Price controls on domestically produced crude oil could not limit this one-time source of approximately half of the higher profits attributable to the embargo. Second, because they did not wish to worsen shortages, the designers of the price controls exempted new, released, and stripper oil, which accounted for 35–40 percent of all domestic crude. This was a wise decision. However, the shortage pushed prices of exempt crude from less than $6 per barrel on the eve of the embargo to nearly $10 by late December; roughly three-fourths of the higher revenues due to this price rise accrued as higher profits to the owners of exempt crude.[34] Third, the FEO, wanting to maintain output in the face of escalating production costs, granted producers of old oil a price rise of $1 per barrel.

It should be stressed that the inefficiencies and inequities of price controls, and their ultimate failure to limit oil company profits, were not the fault of the FEO. It made repeated attempts to remedy these deficiencies. Rather, the fault lies with the basic policy of controlling the price of a product at a level so low that the demand for it far exceeds the supply.

A Remedy

The United States may experience new oil-supply interruptions in the future. If this happens, it may once again decide to implement policies that limit oil company profits in order to gain public acceptance of the necessary austerity measures. The unsatisfactory experience with price controls prompts me to suggest an alternative policy to meet any new sudden shortages in petroleum supply. First, prices of crude oil and refined products should be allowed to rise freely to discourage their consumption, to facilitate the allocation of scarce supplies to their most important uses, and to encourage increased supplies. However, in the event that the oil shortage is so great that it threatens to push prices up to politically intolerable levels, the Federal Energy Administration should have ready for quick implementation a rationing program designed to restrict demands to available supplies. (Rationing should only be used in a real emergency. It should be abolished immediately upon the embargo's close.) Second, to prevent the oil companies from reaping windfall profits from crisis-bred higher prices, Congress should pass legislation that requires the President to impose a temporary excise tax on sales of petroleum products after a formal finding of an energy crisis by the Federal Energy Administration. (It is tempting to recommend the inclusion of a tax on excess profits in this legislation as an alternative presidential option. But I suspect that, as was the case with crude-oil and petroleum-product price controls, an efficient and equitable excess profits tax would be impossible to devise. Furthermore, in practice companies would find many ways to avoid this type of tax.) The temporary excise tax should be set nearly equal to the maximum hike in the prices of petroleum products that Congress feels Americans would tolerate under the circumstances. In order to neutralize the macroeconomic effects of this excise tax and to make it more palatable to the electorate, Congress should require offsetting temporary cuts in federal income and profits taxes, If Congress concludes that poor Americans would bear a disproportionate share of a temporary petroleum excise tax, it should require that these offsetting cuts be proportionately higher for the poor.

LESSONS

In addition to dramatizing the need for long-term policies to reduce U.S. dependence on insecure oil supplies, the largely unsuccessful efforts of the FEO to alleviate the energy crisis of 1973–74 suggest four lessons for mitigating the impact in the event that the United States becomes the target of another petroleum embargo.

First, in a new crisis, the FEA should not be swayed by shrill threats of the magnitude of the petroleum shortages. The embargoing countries have an obvious interest in exaggerating the size of these cutbacks in order to induce swift and total compliance with their demands. The Federal Energy Administration must also carefully discount the exaggeration that arises because each oil-importing country (and each interest group within that country) prepares for the worst by assuming—and claiming—that it will suffer especially severe supply interruptions. It is useful to remember that not all countries (nor all interest groups) can suffer more than the average. The FEO would have had a better appreciation of the real magnitude of the petroleum shortage in the United States during the OAPEC embargo if it had examined trends in oil inventories rather than relying on self-serving claims by the embargoers and domestic oil consumers, or on the too anxious predictions of its own staff.

Second, the Federal Energy Administration should declare publicly that, in future petroleum supply crises, it will not adopt policies that prevent rising petroleum prices. Higher prices should be one of the most powerful tools for obtaining necessary reductions in demand and for allocating scarce supplies to their most important uses. Assuming that Congress passes the appropriate enabling legislation, either excise taxes or excess profit taxes should be used to prevent the oil companies from garnering higher profits from a petroleum embargo.

Third, every effort should be made now—in a crisis-free atmosphere that is favorable to careful design—to pass legislation that would allow the Federal Energy Administration to implement rationing and taxing policies promptly, should they be needed to help alleviate a new oil-supply emergency.

Fourth, to facilitate the third recommendation, the Federal Energy Administration should continue to assign a small permanent staff to the job of guaranteeing that the framework for administering a comprehensive program of petroleum-product rationing is at the ready for fast implementation should another embargo push oil prices to politically intolerable levels. Because any rationing system would be cumbersome to administer and would severely distort resource allocation, this plan should be implemented only after the FEA has reached a formal finding of a likely interruption of supply so large that no other policy would prove adequate for reducing demand quickly and efficiently.

This chapter has explained how many of the FEO's policies actually exacerbated the U.S. energy crisis. Should blame for the ultimate failure of these policies be placed on the FEO's leadership and staff?

The FEO was created after the energy crisis was in full force. No well-considered plans awaited it, and from all sides—Congressional, executive, and public—came urgent calls for bold new policies. Even a well-established agency can flounder in a crisis atmosphere. But FEO was brand new and was, of necessity, in the throes of a massive expansion.

In its new and still unsettled state, the agency especially needed strong day-to-day supervision from the top. Unfortunately, its two top officials, Administrator William Simon and Deputy Administrator John Sawhill, could not supply the requisite supervision because they had to spend most of their time testifying before congressional committees, pleading with various interest groups, or appealing directly to the American people to conserve energy.[35] Because Simon and Sawhill were nearly exhausted by these public relations activities, the direction of day-to-day operations was frequently left to seven assistant administrators and the general counsel. Most of these officials were not accustomed to exercising such significant administrative power and responsibility. Several knew little about energy problems. Also, in the absence of top-level leadership and of established decision-making traditions, these assistants and their nascent staffs inevitably spent considerable time jockeying for internal power.[36]

The FEO's rapid rate of growth also led to staffing problems at lower levels. Even after raids on other governmental agencies, few of the important staff positions were filled with people versed in petroleum matters. Almost no one on the staff had the firsthand experience in the oil industry that might have prevented FEO's complex pricing and allocation regulations from having their frequently undesirable consequences. The obvious way to remedy this particular staff weakness would have been by hiring experienced personnel from the oil industry. However, because both Congress and the FEO's top leadership feared that such employees would unavoidably appear to have conflicts of interest, this alternative was not politically feasible.

In sum, the FEO did suffer severe staffing problems. Nevertheless, it would be fatuous to blame these for the ultimate failure of its regulations. Given the lack of preparation for dealing with any significant interruption in petroleum supply and the impossibility of insulating the FEO from the belligerent demands of politically powerful interest groups, severe staffing problems were unavoidable. In fact, taking account of the conditions under which the staff had to operate, I believe it deserves high marks.[37]

PART TWO

Issues for the Future

CHAPTER THREE
Prospects for Energy Independence

THE 1973–74 OAPEC embargo proved to be a masterstroke for the oil-exporting countries. Besides leading to quintupled oil earnings, it almost immediately established these countries as major powers in determining the future course of world economic and political affairs. Their rulers could no longer be arrogantly dismissed as mere puppets of the economically and militarily powerful industrialized nations. Instead, because of the demonstrated failure of the industrialized nations to cope with the embargo, the leading oil exporters suddenly had to be dealt with as economic and political equals.

The huge successes reaped through bold use of the oil-embargo tactic increases enormously the probability of future repetitions. In an attempt to reduce that probability and its accompanying havoc, on November 7, 1973, President Nixon announced Project Independence: to insure that by 1980 the United States would be able to meet its energy needs ". . . without depending on any foreign energy sources." [1] This chapter assesses the supply-and-demand constraints that will determine whether the United States can achieve energy independence.

Crude oil and natural gas together supply roughly 75 percent of the United States' primary energy needs. Chapter 1 explained why U.S. oil imports soared in the early 1970s. Because domestic production of both crude oil and natural gas had peaked and, without allowing an adjustment period of ten-plus years, other fuels were neither feasible substitutes in many important uses nor available in adequate quantities. Given these facts, total U.S. energy consumption could grow at a 4 percent annual rate from January 1970 to October 1973 only because over the same period oil imports were allowed to rise at a 30 percent annual rate. If the United States is to achieve energy independence, it must reduce the rate of growth of its total energy demand to well below pre-embargo levels while simultaneously accelerating discovery and development of domestic energy.

Few questioned the desirability of Project Independence in the hectic early months of the OAPEC embargo. However, there were two reasons why achieving total energy independence by 1980 was not feasible. First, because it takes several years to commercially introduce and gain widespread usage of most energy-saving consumer durables and capital goods, growing energy demands could be halted immediately only if the U.S. economy suffered recession and stagnancy for the remainder of the 1970s. Second, large increases in energy production from the four most important domestic primary energy sources—crude oil, natural gas, coal, and nuclear—proved to be far more difficult and expensive than President Nixon's advisers anticipated. Moreover, as of mid-1975, significant commercial production from other energy sources such as oil shale, tar sands, synthetic coal derivatives, geothermal, solar, etc., did not appear likely for at least fifteen years. Recognition of these two factors ultimately led to a reformulation of Project Independence's goal: Energy independence was redefined to allow a safe level of oil imports, and the date for achieving this more limited goal was extended to 1985.[2] What are the prospects of successfully completing this redefined Project Independence?

KEY EMPIRICAL PARAMETERS

Table 3.1 lists the Federal Energy Administration's late 1974 estimates of the quantities of the different types of energy that the United States will be consuming in 1985 under four possible scenarios. These scenarios differ according to whether the price of a barrel of crude oil is assumed to be $7 or $11 (in 1974 dollars) between 1974 and 1985 and whether the government initiates several policies designed to spur production of new energy supplies.[3] Given these assumptions, the FEA's specific estimates were calculated in two stages. First, basic supply and cost information was gathered for each type of fuel. Simultaneously, demand estimates were calculated by

Table 3.1
FEA's Estimates of U.S. Fuel Production and Consumption by Source,
1985
(in quadrillion btus)

| | | $7 Oil | | $11 Oil | |
Fuel	1972 Consumption	1985 Base Case	1985 Accelerated Supply	1985 Base Case	1985 Accelerated Supply
Coal	12.5	19.9	17.7	22.9	20.7
	(17.2%)	(18.3%)	(16.2%)	(22.3%)	(19.9%)
Oil	22.4	23.1	30.5	31.3	38.0
	(30.9%)	(21.2%)	(27.9%)	(30.4%)	(36.5%)
Natural gas	22.1	23.9	24.7	24.8	25.5
	(30.5%)	(21.9%)	(22.6%)	(24.1%)	(24.5%)
Hydroelectric and geothermal	2.9	4.8	4.8	4.8	4.8
	(4.0%)	(4.4%)	(4.4%)	(4.7%)	(4.6%)
Nuclear	0.6	12.5	14.7	12.5	14.7
	(0.8%)	(11.5%)	(13.4%)	(12.2%)	(14.1%)
Synthetics	—	—	—	—	0.4
Imports	11.7	24.8	17.1	6.5	0
	(16.1%)	(22.8%)	(15.6%)	(6.3%)	
Totals	72.2	109.0	109.5	102.8	104.1

Source: Federal Energy Administration, *Project Independence Report* (Washington: G.P.O., 1974), Table I-21, p. 46.

estimating total energy demand and then calculating the specific shares of each fuel. Second, the estimates presented in Table 3.1 were the product of an integrating model that calculates:

. . . a feasible set of energy flows that satisfies the final demands for energy. The energy supply activities and the demand prices are adjusted during this market simulation to obtain a balanced solution which is in equilibrium. This equilibrium balance is found at the point at which no consuming sector would be willing to pay more for an additional unit of any energy product and no supplier would provide an additional unit of any energy product for less than the prevailing market price.[4]

The methodological sophistication of the Federal Energy Administration's *Project Independence Report* is impressive. Of particular importance is the explicit recognition that future consumption and production trends in the different energy subsectors depend on assumed future prices and are intimately intertwined. Nevertheless, primarily because the demand and supply data underlying the *Project Independence* study is hopelessly inadequate, many of its specific conclusions are dubious.[5] Elaboration follows.

Crude Oil

Crude-oil production has been falling steadily since peaking at an average of 9.6 million barrels per day in 1970. Daily U.S. crude-oil production averaged only 8.5 million barrels during 1974. Roughly 83 percent (or 7.1 million barrels per day) came from onshore wells located in the "inland 48" states. The remaining 17 percent came from the Outer Continental Shelf.

If the United States is to reduce its dependence on imported oil, sharply higher outputs from domestic sources will be necessary. However, unless there are large additions to presently discovered recoverable crude-oil reserves, U.S. crude-oil output must continue to fall. Today there is a spirited debate about whether there are now sufficient undiscovered but ultimately recoverable crude-oil reserves to make possible any sizable expansion of U.S. crude-oil output. Table 3.2 reports three authoritative estimates. Most optimistic is the United States Geological Survey's (USGS) 1974 estimate that there are 200–400 billion barrels of undiscovered but ultimately economically recoverable crude-oil reserves within the United States. The validity of this estimate depends crucially on the assumption that potential but still unexplored oil-bearing formations contain 0.5 to 1.0 times as much oil as comparable volumes in explored formations.[6] Critics of the USGS, most notably geologist M. King Hubbert, attack this procedure as almost certainly leading to overly optimistic results when applied to the inland 48 states because it ignores the fact that the oil industry has always drilled the best prospects first.[7] This explains why U.S. onshore oil-discovery rates fell from an average of 240 barrels per foot drilled during 1860–1920 to around 20–30 barrels per foot drilled in recent years.

Table 3.2
Three Estimates of U.S. Undiscovered Recoverable Crude
Oil and Natural Gas Liquids

Source of Estimate	Estimated Undiscovered Recoverable Crude Oil and Natural Gas Liquids (billion barrels)		
	Inland 48 States	Offshore and Alaska	Total
USGS	110–220	90–180	200–400
Mobil	13	75	88
Hubbert			29 *

Source: Science magazine, July 12, 1974, p. 127. Volumes shown for USGS and Mobil include natural gas liquids.
* Hubbert's estimate is assumed to be crude oil only.

The USGS critics have a strong argument. There can be no doubt that, with the important exceptions of the Alaskan North Slope and large areas of the Outer Continental Shelf (OCS), those areas of the United States thought to have commercial quantities of petroleum have already been heavily explored. In general, large fields are easier to find than small ones. Hence, most of the larger and more productive oil fields in these heavily explored areas have almost certainly been found and developed, and most of those not already exhausted are currently being produced.

Most of the crude oil already produced in the United States has come from a few large fields:

. . . 250 of the 60,000-odd reservoirs in the United States account for over 65% of domestic production to date, 75% of the API[American Petroleum Institute] recoverable reserves and over 60% of the already discovered remaining oil in place. And even within this sample of large fields, the distribution of volume is highly skewed toward the 100 largest fields.[8]

In large part because of the steady deterioration of the potential oil-bearing formations still awaiting exploration in onshore areas, since 1971 oil companies have not been able to develop new supplies of inland 48 oil sufficient to offset the fall in output resulting from the steady depletion of currently producing fields. In sum, available evi-

dence suggests that the USGS' 1974 estimate of the inland 48's undiscovered but recoverable crude-oil reserves is of the wrong magnitude.[9]

In addition to the magnitude of presently undiscovered crude-oil
reserves, future U.S. oil output will be determined by the success in
finding new supplies and the ability to extract what is found. These
two parameters are, in turn, largely determined by the interplay of
economic and technological factors. Sharp post-embargo hikes in the
prices of "new," "released," and "stripper" crude oil will encourage more intensive recovery of oil from currently producing stripper
fields and new production from some previously uneconomic sources.
Soaring prices also triggered additional large investments to discover
and develop new supplies of domestic oil. Thus, drilling statistics for
the United States show that during 1974 the number of wells drilled
jumped 29 percent.[10] In contrast, present "old" oil-price controls
discourage investments to exploit large quantities of already developed reserves more intensively. Even worse, because there is some
prospect that these pernicious controls will be eliminated, there is an
additional incentive to reduce present output of old oil in the hopes
that it can be sold later at a far higher price. The net effect of sharply
higher post-embargo prices for exempt crude oil but the continuance
of low pre-embargo prices on old oil is probably slight. Hence, given
maintenance of both policies, I would expect output from presently
established inland 48 producing regions to continue to decline
through the 1970s. However, on the assumption that real prices of
exempt domestic crude oil remain at mid-1975 levels and that present
controls mandating low old oil prices are eliminated, the resultant additional investments should reduce and, within just a few years, halt
the decline in U.S. oil output from these traditional areas of onshore
oil production.

Because most of the best (i.e., high volume) "inland 48" fields
have already been found, crude-oil production from these areas seems
unlikely to increase even if old oil-price controls are abolished.[11]
Any large net increments to present U.S. oil reserves will probably
be found in presently unexplored areas of the Alaskan North Slope
and the Outer Continental Shelf (OCS).

Petroleum geologists are fond of reciting the old saw, "Big oil runs in schools." That is, when one large oil field is discovered, others are often found nearby. The plethora of large oil discoveries in British and Norweigan North Sea waters since 1970, when the discovery of North Sea oil was first announced, attest to the wisdom of this dictum.

The proved reserves of Northern Alaska's Prudhoe Bay oil field are 9.6 billion barrels. Discovered in 1968 after a relatively modest (by present standards) exploratory effort, Prudhoe Bay is far and away the largest and most productive oil field ever found in North America. Its owners expect that this single field will be producing roughly 1.6 million barrels per day (or nearly 20 percent of 1974 U.S. output) in the early 1980s.

Normally, a successful discovery like the one at Prudhoe Bay would have immediately precipitated a huge surge of additional exploration aimed at finding crude oil and natural gas in promising nearby geological formations. There were two reasons why this did not happen. First, many of the most promising North Slope areas have never been leased for oil exploration. Most important is the United States Navy's huge 24-million-acre Naval Petroleum Reservation Number 4 which almost borders the Prudhoe Bay Field. Even though N.P.R. Number 4 apparently contains several promising large geological structures and Congress initially created it to provide the United States with a source of emergency petroleum supplies, as of mid-1975 this potentially huge petroleum source had not been explored systematically because of Congressional reluctance to authorize funds of the necessary magnitude. In addition to not exploring N.P.R. Number 4, North Slope exploration was also reduced because of the added uncertainty introduced as a result of the environmental litigation that caused a long delay in starting the trans-Alaskan pipeline. In sum, more than seven years after the discovery of Prudhoe Bay, all estimates of its oil potential must still be regarded as speculative.

Commercial oil production from U.S. offshore waters began in the late 1940s. Most of the 1.5 million barrels per day of offshore oil produced during 1974 came from a subset of the approximately 7 million acres of federal OCS lands leased prior to 1970; the rest came almost entirely from state-owned offshore lands. The federal government held eight large and three small OCS lease sales from 1970 to 1974. Table 3.3 shows that companies leased roughly 4 million acres at these OCS sales in return for bonuses totaling more than $11 billion. Because, assuming the luck of early discovery, the time lag from lease sale to significant production is three to six years in the Gulf of Mexico, in 1975 the United States was just beginning to receive significant quantities of crude oil and natural gas from the large post-1970 OCS petroleum leases. However, if the oil companies are to recover their mammoth $11 billion-plus 1970–74 OCS leasing investments, the oil flow will have to exceed 1 million barrels per day when fully developed.[12]

Table 3.3
Federal Outer Continental Shelf Lease Sales From
1970 Through 1974

Date of Sale	Location	Acres Leased	Total Bonus Paid
July 21, 1970	La.	44,642	$ 97,769,013
Dec. 15, 1970	La.	551,398	846,784,660
Nov. 4, 1971	La.	37,222	96,304,523
Sept. 12, 1972	La.	290,321	585,827,925
Dec. 19, 1972	La.	535,874	1,665,519,631
June 19, 1973	Tex.-La.	547,173	1,591,397,380
Dec. 20, 1973	Miss.-Ala.-Fla.	485,397	1,491,065,231
Mar. 28, 1974	La.	421,218	2,092,510,854
Sept. 29, 1974	Tex.	565,112	1,471,851,831
July 30, 1974 [a]	La.-Tex.	100,241	30,236,800
Oct. 16, 1974	La.	634,832	1,427,242,454
TOTALS		4,213,430	$11,396,510,302

Source: U.S. Department of Interior, Bureau of Land Management, New Orleans Office, *Outer Continental Shelf Statistical Summary.*

[a] The acreage offered in the July 30, 1974 lease sale had been offered for sale at earlier lease sales. This land had either received no bids or bids that the Interior Department had rejected as too low.

Roughly 6.5 million acres of federal OCS lands were under lease at the close of 1974.[13] All were located either in the Gulf of Mexico or off the California coast. By U.S. standards presently producing OCS fields are relatively large, and, excluding lease bonus payments, low-cost sources.[14] As of January 1, 1975 the United States still had not leased roughly 79 million acres of potentially productive OCS lands located in the Gulf of Mexico and off the California coast at depths less than 200 meters; the same waters contain another 160 million acres of unleased OCS lands at depths between 200 and 2500 meters.[15] Prior to 1975 very few of the OCS oil and gas leases had been issued for acreage in areas beyond 200 meters deep.

Drilling has never been allowed in the United States' massive landholdings in other OCS waters. However, the oil industry has developed many geophysical techniques for assessing a region's petroleum prospects prior to drilling. Using these techniques, many companies operating in the western Gulf of Mexico in the early 1970s were successful in identifying large natural-gas formations. On the basis of cursory geophysical studies, the OCS waters of the Gulf of Alaska (off southern Alaska) and the Atlantic seaboard are thought to be potentially large petroleum sources. Indeed, present indications are that oil-bearing structures in these frontier areas will be both far larger and less complex than their Gulf of Mexico counterparts.[16] Unfortunately, geophysical techniques are not foolproof. To illustrate, goaded on by promising geophysical studies a consortium of three companies paid a $623.4 million bonus in December 1973 for rights to just six tracts on the Destin anticline in the eastern Gulf of Mexico. After drilling seven dry wildcats at a cost exceeding $15 million, the Destin partners announced that they had no plans for more drilling.[17] The Destin failure illustrates that some drilling remains a prerequisite for informed estimates of a region's petroleum potential.

The Interior Department has announced plans to accelerate the leasing of OCS lands for the remainder of the 1970s. Initially most of this will be in the traditional areas of U.S. offshore production: in the Gulf of Mexico and off the coast of California at depths less than 200 meters. Because most of the best prospects in these traditional OCS areas have already been leased (many between 1970 and 1974), their output seems likely to peak around 1980. Large lease sales can be anticipated in both the Gulf of Alaska and off the Atlantic coast prior to 1980. Until much more detailed geophysical work has been done and a considerable number of wells have been drilled, any estimates of oil production from these frontier OCS areas must be regarded as highly speculative. However, there is a reasonable chance that they will become a significant source of future U.S. oil supplies.

Table 3.4 presents the Federal Energy Administration's *Project Independence Report* estimates of the sources of U.S. domestic oil production in 1985 for each of the four scenarios previously de-

Table 3.4
Sources of U.S. Oil Production in 1985
(million barrels per day)

Source	1974 Production	FEA's Estimates of 1985 Production			
		$7 Oil		$11 Oil	
		Base Case	Accelerated Supply	Base Case	Accelerated Supply
"Inland 48"	6.9	4.2	4.3	7.4	6.3
Alaska (excl. North Slope)	0.2	0.1	0.1	0.5	0.8
Alaska North Slope	—	2.5	2.5	2.5	2.5
Alaska N.P.R. Number 4	—	—	2.0	—	2.0
OCS	1.4	2.1	3.6	2.1	3.6
Shale oil	—	0.3	0.3	0.3	1.0
Tar sands	—	—	—	0.1	0.3
Total	8.5	9.2	12.8	12.9	16.5

Sources: Federal Energy Administration, *Project Independence Report* (Washington: G.P.O., 1974), Tables I-22, p. 47. and II-9, p. 83.

scribed. Like all estimates of 1985 U.S. oil output, their accuracy is dependent upon the accuracy of the values assumed for three key parameters:

1. future oil-price levels and the linkage between oil prices and levels of domestic output;
2. the size, location, and timing of future sales of federal oil land leases;
3. the true crude-oil potential of the United States' petroleum areas— especially the Alaskan North Slope (including N.P.R. Number 4) and the virgin waters of the Outer Continental Shelf.

All assumptions about these values are highly speculative. To illustrate: Future oil prices may not be in the $7-$11 range (see chapter

5). Econometric and qualitative estimates of the price elasticity (i.e., responsiveness) of U.S. crude-oil supplies differ substantially and past estimates have usually been far wide of the mark. Moreover, because post-OAPEC embargo oil prices are far beyond the range experienced earlier, even valid statistical relationships would be inappropriate if deduced from pre-embargo data. Also, if recent history offers any guide, the Interior Department will repeatedly revise its OCS leasing plans and efforts to implement its plans will be frequently thwarted. Even if they are not thwarted, the true potential of the United States' unexplored petroleum areas is unknown. In sum, because they are premised on an inadequate and essentially arbitrary factual base, all attempts to project the level of U.S. oil supplies more than three to five years into the future should be viewed skeptically. Given this caveat, my best guess is that U.S. actual daily crude-oil output will range between 10 and 13 million barrels in 1985.

Natural Gas

Crude oil and natural gas are found in similar (frequently the same) geological structures and tend to be produced by companies using roughly the same technology. Hence, the basic economic, physical, and technical factors that will determine the level of the United States' future natural gas production are analogous to those factors determining future crude-oil production. It follows that the accuracy of any estimate of 1985 U.S. natural gas output is chiefly dependent upon the accuracy of the values assumed for three key parameters:

1. future natural gas price levels and the linkage between natural gas prices and levels of domestic output;
2. the size, location, and timing of future sales of federal petroleum lands;
3. the true natural-gas potential of the United States' unexplored petroleum areas.

Because FPC price ceilings have kept the price of most natural gas far below market-clearing levels since the early 1960s (see chapter 1), future natural gas prices will probably be the most important determinant of future supplies.

In early 1975 the Federal Power Commission allowed a price of

50-cents per Mcf (1,000 cubic feet) on new sales of natural gas to interstate markets; simultaneously, the price of new sales of natural gas
in unregulated intrastate markets ranged between $1.50 and $2 per
Mcf. Crude oil and natural gas are close substitutes in many uses. A
price of 50 cents per Mcf for natural gas is equivalent to a price of
$2.80 per barrel for crude oil; in contrast, a price of $2 per Mcf for
natural gas is equivalent to a price of $11.20 per barrel for crude oil.
The price of new domestic crude oil was about $11 per barrel in early
1975.

Table 3.5 presents the Federal Energy Administration's estimates
of 1985 U.S. natural gas production for a variety of assumed natural
gas prices. Assuming, as the FEA does, that crude-oil prices will
range between $7 and $11 per barrel, the deregulated price of natural
gas would range between $1.25 and $2 per Mcf. But the FEA's 1985
natural gas estimates show almost no supply responsiveness to natural-gas prices about 80 cents per Mcf. The obvious inference
(though the FEA does not make it) is that deregulation of natural gas
prices will not add appreciably to U.S. natural-gas supplies.

Table 3.5
FEA's Estimates of U.S. Natural Gas Production *
(trillion cubic feet)

Assumed Wellhead Price	1974	1985
$0.40	20.187	16.116
$0.60	20.335	23.288
$0.80	20.335	24.772
$1.00	20.335	24.785
$2.00	20.335	24.805

* Assumes price of oil is $11.

Source: Federal Energy Administration, *Project Independence Report*
(Washington: G.P.O., 1974), Tables II-12, p. 93 and II-13, p. 94.

The FEA's forecast of future natural gas supplies at prices above
80 cents per Mcf should be dismissed as implausibly low because it
ignores the fact that drilling rates would soar at higher deregulated
prices. Forecasts derived from a far more sophisticated and compre-

hensive model developed by Professors Paul MacAvoy and Robert Pyndyck suggest that natural gas could be supplying the equivalent of as much as 5 million barrels of crude oil (i.e., more than 10 trillion cubic feet of natural gas per year) over and above the FEA forecast.[18] The MacAvoy-Pyndyck forecast is, of course, also subject to uncertainty. However, all of the recent natural-gas supply forecasts reviewed by an M.I.T. study group are significantly higher than the FEA's.[19] After reviewing available evidence, my best guess of 1985 U.S. natural-gas production (assuming wellhead prices are decontrolled prior to 1978) is that it will be at least 4 trillion cubic feet higher than the FEA's *Project Independence Report* forecasts.

Coal

Discussions of the American coal industry tend to dwell ad nauseam on two facts. First, that the United States has enormous minable coal reserves, sufficient to last more than 800 years at current consumption rates. Second, that coal's share of the total U.S. energy market has tumbled from 90-plus percent in 1900 to only 17 percent in 1974. Given just these two facts, the path to achieving energy independence appears deceptively simple: The United States should adopt policies to encourage greater coal production and consumption and thereby reverse its declining share of the U.S. energy market.

The above analysis requires three qualifications. First, the chief reason why coal's market share has plummeted since 1900 is that it is a very inflexible fuel—primarily because all coal users must maintain large and usually dirty on-site storage facilities. Coal's lack of flexibility compared to natural gas and refined oil products severely limits the markets it can hope to supply. Ninety percent of all coal is presently consumed in just two large-scale uses: generation of electricity and metal smelting. Since the disappearance of the steam locomotive, none is used in the large transportation sector. Unless synthetic natural gas or oil made from coal becomes commercially feasible, it will not be practical to substitute large quantities of coal for petroleum in other uses. Hence, accelerated development of coal supplies is not sufficient to render the United States independent of foreign energy.

Second, because coal combustion produces relatively more undesirable air emissions (especially sulphur but also particulates) than combustion of other fossil fuels, there is even some doubt that utilities will be allowed to burn large additional quantities to produce electricity. The FEA's *Project Independence Report* blithely assumes that coal's air-pollution problems can be circumvented by using stack gas scrubbers.[20] However, in view of the fact that many utilities have challenged both the effectiveness and reliability of commercial scrubbers—and have actively resisted installing these expensive and still unproven devices—this assumption may be wrong.[21]

Third, if stack gas scrubbers cannot be used, electric utilities will be forced either to burn low-sulphur coal or to turn to alternative fuels. Low-sulphur coal is in short supply east of the Mississippi. Thus new contracts for low-sulphur Eastern coal specify prices that are closely related to the price of comparable quantities of residual fuel oil. Large increases in supplies of Eastern low-sulphur coal may be impossible and will certainly be expensive.

Low-sulphur coal is abundant in the Western United States. However, Western coal is far from major electricity markets and has a relatively low energy content. Hence, transportation costs will be high. Also, before output can be expanded to desired levels, Congress and the President must agree to policies regulating strip mining and the leasing of Western coal lands. After bitter debate, no agreement was reached on these issues in the first half of 1975. In brief, because of very real environmental and political problems, the mere existence of massive coal reserves is not sufficient to guarantee that the United States can have ready access to large new low-cost coal supplies simply by developing the requisite number of new mines.

Coal is not the panacea that will allow the United States to achieve energy independence prior to 1985. However, this does not mean that there is no role for coal to play. First, coal can and should be used to fuel new electricity-generating plants, even if this results in some deterioration in air quality. Second, if natural gas wellhead price controls are eliminated, it will be profitable to ship Western coal to Texas, Louisiana, Oklahoma, and Arkansas where it can be substituted for large quantities of natural gas currently burned as boiler fuel. The displaced natural gas (equivalent to several hundred thousand barrels per day of crude oil) could then be sold to gas-short interstate pipelines. Since refined oil products are the closest substitute to natural gas and since U.S. demands for both natural gas and crude oil are already far greater than domestic supplies, this substitution of coal for natural gas would ultimately lead to reduced oil imports.

Nuclear Fuels

Nuclear fuels are even less flexible than coal. Their only commercial use is to generate electricity. By year-end 1974 the United States had 53 operational commercial nuclear reactors with a combined capacity of 32,000 megawatts; they accounted for 7 percent of the nation's total electricity-generating capacity. *The Project Independence Report* projects that roughly 200 nuclear plants with a combined capacity of 204,000 megawatts will be necessary by 1985.[22] If this projection is correct, nuclear power plants will account for approximately 22 percent of U.S. electricity-generating capacity in 1985. To support this level of nuclear capacity, the United States would have to sharply increase its uranium exploration and development and its capacity to enrich these ores. This would be expensive but feasible.

There are at least four reasons why expansion of the U.S. nuclear electricity-generating capacity probably will not and should not rise to the heights the FEA projects. First, because of rising construction and financing costs coupled with falling electricity demand growth, electric utilities announced plans to abandon or delay projects to build roughly 120,000 megawatts of nuclear capacity in 1974 (see chapter 8). Second, considerable controversy surrounds the issue of nuclear plant safety. A prestigious study group jointly sponsored by the Atomic Energy Commission and the National Science Foundation concluded that the probability of a major accident with light-water reactors releasing radioactivity seems small. However, its "quantification deserves more attention within the reactor safety community than it has received up until now." [23] Third, the opportunities for terrorists to engage in nuclear sabotage or blackmail may not be negligible. Fourth, the problem of safe and permanent disposal of nuclear wastes remains to be solved.

Chapter 4 discusses the problems of nuclear safety, sabotage, and waste disposal in more detail. It concludes that these nuclear-related problems are potentially many times more severe than the environmental problems associated with increased production and consumption of the three conventional fossil fuels. However, nuclear power does hold considerable promise in the more distant future. Hence, I recommend that the United States continue to finance current levels of nuclear power research but that it adopt a go-slow approach to its commercial introduction.

Other Fuels

The United States consumes negligible amounts of other fuels. However, optimistic claims about the ultimate potential of oil shale, tar sands, synthetic coal derivatives, geothermal power, solar power, and fusion abound. Trying to assess the ultimate importance of energy from these sources is beyond the scope of this study. However, it can be said with assurance that regardless of what policy measures are taken, they will supply trivial amounts of energy prior to 1985: A sustained controlled fusion reaction has yet to be achieved—fusion power is unlikely to be commercial within 25 years of that breakthrough. Most presently undeveloped domestic geothermal sources are poisoned with highly corrosive salts; a commercial technology for generating electricity with corrosive steam does not yet exist. Because solar power is very dispersed, the collection of large quantities is prohibitively expensive, using known techniques. For at least 20 years advocates of oil shale, tar sands, and synthetic coal derivatives have asserted that large-scale production would be profitable if the price of crude oil were just slightly higher. Following the enormous crude-oil price hike during 1973–74, work did begin on several commercial plants. However, within just a few months it became apparent that the cost of building the monstrous, capital-intensive plants necessary for producing these products had been seriously underestimated.[24] As a result, several companies have backed out of these ventures; other projects have been deferred. A technological breakthrough (e.g., in situ recovery of oil shale and tar sands) that will enable profitable commercial production from these sources may soon occur. However, since it takes five to ten years to build these plants, significant amounts of oil from these sources are not likely to be produced prior to 1985.

Future Energy Supplies

Assuming an $11 price for crude oil, the FEA estimates that aggregate U.S. energy production will range between 96.3 and 104.1 quadrillion Btu in 1985.[25] To achieve this result, U.S. energy production will have to grow roughly 5 percent annually from 1976 to 1985.

The foregoing examination of future prospects for the four most important fuels suggests that the FEA's projections of 1985 domestic supplies of coal, crude oil, and nuclear power are probably too high whereas its natural gas projection (assuming decontrol of wellhead prices) is too low. On balance, I suspect that the annual rate of growth in total U.S. energy production from 1976 to 1985 will average 3 to 4 percent. This implies that U.S. energy production will range between 80 and 90 quadrillion Btu in 1985. If domestic energy output is near the low end of this range, total energy independence is possible only if average demand growth is held to less than 1 percent annually. If crude oil imports are allowed to stay at their 1974 levels or if domestic output is near the high end of this range, U.S. energy demands can grow 2 percent annually.

Future Energy Demands

U.S. energy demands were growing 4 percent annually in the years just prior to the OAPEC embargo. Regardless of what 1985 supply projections are used, continuation of this rate of demand growth would make it impossible to achieve total independence from imported oil. However, as long as the deflated prices of all types of energy stay at their far higher post-embargo levels, it is unlikely that U.S. energy demands will again grow at this 4 percent rate for a sustained period.[26]

Prior to the embargo, the present generation of Americans had never experienced large energy price hikes. Indeed, since the end of World War II the trend in deflated energy prices was steadily downward. Hence, quantitative estimates of the price responsiveness of U.S. energy demands deduced from pre-embargo data probably have little relevance for predicting post-embargo consumption. Rather than repeat these estimates, it is more useful to describe qualitatively the likely effects on demand of persistent sharply higher energy price levels.

Historically, U.S. energy demands have grown roughly as fast as real gross national product (GNP).[27] The historical constancy of this relationship has frequently been explained as being entailed by technology. The argument goes as follows: Energy is a key input required to produce many of the goods and services comprising GNP; therefore, technologic constraints require that energy consumption grow roughly as fast as real GNP. The chief flaw in this argument is the failure to consider the likely effects of higher prices.

Because over the past century (prior to 1973) the relative price of energy fell, it is not surprising that many chose to substitute increased energy inputs for other, relatively more expensive, goods and productive factors. If, instead, relative energy prices had risen, there would have been fewer of these substitutions, and the observed rate of growth of energy consumption would have been less. Evidence from intercountry comparisons suggests that these price-induced savings could be large. To illustrate:

1. Coking coal is much cheaper in the United States than in Japan. In part because of these cost differences, the American steel industry consumes roughly 30 percent more coal per ton of steel produced.
2. Largely because of excise tax differences, most refined oil products cost roughly twice as much in Western Europe as in the United States. At least partially as a result of these cost differences (and the European practice of placing much heavier excise taxes on larger new cars), in the early 1970s the typical European motorist drove a car that got roughly twice as many miles per gallon as the car driven by his American counterpart.

These dramatic intercountry differences suggest that it is a mistake to view the level of real GNP as the sole determinant of the level of energy demand; relative price levels are also important.

The relative prices of all types of energy rose sharply in late 1973 and additional price rises were anticipated. Initially, even this large price rise caused only a slight reduction in energy demand because there were only a few short-run substitutes. To illustrate, higher energy prices prompted many consumers to take steps to reduce home and office temperatures, drive less, and turn off lights in unoccupied rooms. However, the total reduction in energy demand as a result of these initial price-induced measures was slight—primarily because the costs of larger reductions were regarded, in most cases, as too high. Homes and offices were judged too uncomfortable when their temperatures fell much below 68°F; suburban families found it inconvenient to spend several additional minutes each day walking, riding bikes, or waiting for buses; and few of us were willing to unplug our instant-on color TVs at the close of each viewing day.

As the years pass the price-induced fall in energy demand will grow far larger because additional and better energy-saving substitutions become possible. For example, those buying new homes and offices will opt for more insulation, storm windows, and more efficient furnaces. Growing numbers of car buyers are choosing to trade size, power, and perhaps even styling for greater fuel economy; moreover, automobile companies are building more efficient engines and lighter cars. And, new solid-state TVs use far less electricity than the vacuum-tube models they replace. In sum, even though energy prices have risen sharply, the linkage between levels of energy demand and GNP must remain rather tight for the remainder of the 1970s because of a lack of economic substitutes. However, it will loosen considerably as the 1980s pass because a greater variety of energy-saving substitutions will become feasible. Since the main uses of energy are for powering, transporting, or heating relatively long-lived capital assets and durable consumer goods, the time required to complete most of the transition from short-run to long-run should be at least 10 to 15 years.

As of mid-1975 the United States appears to be coming out of its worst postwar recession. As a result, real GNP seems likely to grow at above-average rates for most of the remainder of the 1970s. Hence, it seems likely that total U.S. energy demands will grow at an average annual rate of 3 to 4 percent from 1976 to 1980. However, by 1980 many significant energy-saving substitutions will have been made. Hence, assuming that the real price of energy does not fall from mid-1975 levels, I would expect that growth in U.S. energy demands may average only 2 percent in the 1980s.

Suppose U.S. energy demands do grow at roughly the rates just projected. Then U.S. energy consumption will range between 95 and 105 quadrillion Btu in 1985. If total domestic energy production is between 80 and 90 quadrillion Btu, the United States' 1985 oil imports will be between 2 and 10 million barrels per day. Oil imports were 6.5 million barrels per day in 1974.

SUMMARY

Assuming maintenance of mid-1975 or higher foreign crude-oil prices, gradual decontrol of "old" oil prices and interstate natural gas prices, and no unexpected delays in developing new petroleum sources in northern Alaska or the Outer Continental Shelf or new coal mines in the West, U.S. oil imports should not rise appreciably between 1975 and 1985.[28] Whether this result is judged satisfactory depends on one's assessment of how insecure future oil imports are likely to be and what are the likely costs of policies designed to achieve even greater import reductions. These issues are addressed in the remainder of this book.

CHAPTER FOUR

Energy and the Environment: The Need for Priorities

BARRING CONTINUOUS economic stagnation, the United States' energy consumption must grow, albeit more slowly than in pre-embargo years, until at least the early 1980s.[1] Hence, reduced dependence on oil imports is possible only if there is increased production from domestic energy sources. Unfortunately, with the exception of natural gas, increased production of domestic energy entails varying degrees of environmental degradation and, in the case of nuclear power, increased exposure to severe public safety risks.

Energy-related environmental and public safety problems merit serious and sustained public consideration.[2] However, in recent years environmentalists have damaged their cause by appearing to attack all feasible options (over the 1975–85 time span) for creating sizable increments in U.S. energy supplies. Certain environmental and safety costs must be incurred if the United States is to prevent an ever-growing dependence on potentially insecure oil imports. Environmentalists would strengthen their effectiveness if they would accept this fact, then ascertain an environmental ranking of the different feasible energy supply options, and finally lobby to persuade energy policymakers to devote most attention to accelerating energy production from those sources posing the least environmental and public safety risks. America's future energy needs will be supplied at unnecessarily high environmental and public safety costs if decision makers are allowed to ignore these priorities.

This chapter was co-authored by Sean Randolph.

ENVIRONMENTAL COSTS

Over the 1975–85 time span the United States has the economic resources and technological capability to increase energy output from a variety of domestic sources: crude oil and natural gas from the Outer Continental Shelf (and northern Alaska), coal, nuclear power, and oil shale. What are the relative environmental and public safety costs of these different energy supply options?

Outer Continental Shelf Crude Oil

Expansion of Outer Continental Shelf (OCS) crude-oil production would increase both the incidence of accidental spills and the level of chronic pollution that normally accompanies offshore operations. In the aftermath of the 1969 blowout of a well in the Santa Barbara channel, many environmentalists argued that these costs were so high that all new OCS drilling should be suspended. Because a large number of Americans depend heavily on aquatic and shoreline resources to supply physical and recreational needs, fears of large oil spills and chronic pollution from OCS production platforms are certainly legitimate. Nevertheless, when compared with the sizable environmental and safety costs that are by-products of the production of equivalent amounts of domestic energy from coal, nuclear power, or oil shale, increased OCS crude-oil production is the environmentally preferable option. In fact, when judged by environmental criteria, higher OCS crude-oil production is even preferable to higher oil imports.

The biological and physical effects of an oil spill depend on three critical variables: the chemical composition of the crude or refined oil, the dispersion of the spill, and the persistence of oil in the affected region. Crude oil is composed of three different types of hydrocarbons: aliphatics, alicyclics, and aromatics. The aromatics are particularly toxic and are thought to contain carcinogens.

Crude oil begins to weather (i.e., lose its toxic properties) upon its release into water. Weathering is the result of evaporation, dissolution, microbial and chemical oxidation, and photochemical reactions that continually alter the oil's chemical structure. The different hydrocarbons weather at different rates: the greater part of most crude-oil spills weathers within two days; however, recent research has established that because the relatively more toxic aromatics are water soluble, they mix into the water column and persist in the environment for an extended period.

Two types of emulsions are commonly formed in oil spills: the first, "oil-in-water," is a multitude of small droplets that tend to disperse over a large area; the second, "water-in-oil," forms a viscous floating mass frequently called a "chocolate mousse." An oil spill thus appears as a substantial glob surrounded by a thinner film. The actual pattern of surface fractionation has an important effect on the rate at which any oil spill weathers.

In sum, because of wind, waves, currents, and tides, spilled oil spreads at varying rates far beyond its original locale. It fractionates on the water's surface and undergoes weathering that significantly alters its chemical composition. Although the greater part of the toxic compounds are removed in the weathering process, some remain in the slick and in the surrounding water column and sediments. Weathered oil ultimately either settles into marine sediments, is ingested by marine organisms, or attaches to rocks, plants, animals, or the coastline.

Available data show that the persistence of oil pollution varies with different marine habitats. Studies following the 1969 Santa Barbara spill found oil still present in sediments one and one-half years after the original blowout; weathered oil found in the upper intertidal zone four years later was believed to be from the same spill.[3]

A study made in the aftermath of the 1969 West Falmouth, Massachusetts, tanker spill concluded:

> In May 1970, eight months after the spill, oil essentially unaltered in chemical characteristics could still be recovered from the sediments of the most heavily polluted areas. By the end of the first year . . . bacterial degradation of the oil was noted at all locations. . . . Yet only partial detoxification of the sediments had occurred, since the bacteria attacked the least toxic hydrocarbons first. The more toxic aromatic hydrocarbons remained in the sediments.[4]

Available evidence suggests that oil discharged into a marine environment can be expected to persist at least two to three years on rocky and sandy shores, and four to five years in salt marshes and the sediments of the offshore bottom.[5]

How toxic are oil spills? Following the 1969 Santa Barbara spill marine life in the upper intertidal zone was virtually eliminated by the oil slick, and repopulation was hindered by heavy oil layers on the rocks. However, inspection of selected species (including limpets, mussels, and barnacles) in other zones discovered apparently normal breeding and recovery taking place. The quality and quantity of fish appeared to be only slightly affected. Damage to marine flora (with the exception of intertidal surf grass) was slight. But damage to aquatic birds was heavy—oil coated their feathers causing loss of buoyancy and insulation and hampering their ability to fly. When they preened their feathers, these birds ingested some toxic fractions and coated their internal organs with oil. Of 1,653 birds taken to cleaning stations following the Santa Barbara spill, only 198 were alive three months later.

Damage to marine mammals as a result of the Santa Barbara spill remains a matter of dispute. A number of dead seals, porpoises, and whales were washed ashore coated with oil. However, it was never established that contact with oil caused their deaths.

Because it occurred near the Woods Hole Oceanographic Institution, more detailed data on biological damage are available for the 1969 West Falmouth spill:

> Massive, immediate destruction of marine life occurred offshore during the first few days after the accident. Affected were a wide range of fish, shellfish, worms, crabs and other crustaceans, and invertebrates. Bottom-living fish and lobsters were killed. . . . Trawls made in ten feet of water soon after the spill showed that 95% of the animals recovered were dead. . . . [T]hese observations demonstrate that chronic pollution can result from a single spill, that the decimation of marine life can extend to new regions long after the initial spill, and that, once poisoned the sea bottom may remain toxic to animals for long time periods. . . . Our investigation demonstrated that the spill produced . . . destruction of fishery resources and continued harm to fisheries for a long period after the accident.[6]

Because damage from oil spills is very real, it is important to assess how spills may be prevented and, when not prevented, may be cleaned up in a way that minimizes environmental damage.

Blowouts, the most devastating form of crude oil production accident, can occur in both the drilling and production phases of an offshore operation. Offshore drilling methods are similar to those used onshore. The wellhole is made by using a rotary drill, which consists of a drill bit on the end of a string of drill pipe. Cuttings from the bit are removed from the wellhole with drilling mud, a fluid which is pumped down through the string, out of the bit, and back to the surface by way of the annular space between the central drill string and the bore hole. Besides eliminating cuttings, the drilling mud also helps to prevent blowouts by counterweighing subsurface pressures.

An oil well is successful if the bit passes through porous rock formations containing commercial quantities of crude oil or natural gas. The difference between surface and subsurface pressures is usually sufficient to force a flow of crude oil or natural gas up the wellbore. This inflow is controlled by the countervailing weight of the column of drilling mud in the wellbore. During normal drilling operations the pressures of the hydrocarbons and drilling mud are balanced. However, sometimes as a formation is penetrated, there is a sudden surge of pressure into the wellbore (called a kick). To prevent a blowout when a kick occurs, additional drilling mud must be rushed into the hole in order to offset the surge of pressure. An accurate flow of information concerning bore-hole pressure, mud volume, and mud circulation is essential for detecting and controlling those variations in drilling conditions that could lead to blowouts. Use of improved monitoring devices can help reduce the incidence of blowouts.

In addition to drilling mud and accurate monitoring devices, a key device for blowout control is the blowout preventer stack, a series of three valves designed either to close around the drill string and seal off the annular space or to totally close the bore hole. The blowout preventers are activated only when drilling mud fails. First, two preventers close around the drill pipe. If these prove inadequate to control the pressure, the third preventer crimps the pipe and closes the wellhole. The third preventer is used only as a last resort because, after the pipe is crimped, it is often necessary to abandon a well that cost up to $10 million to drill. As long as they are properly maintained and competently operated, blowout preventer stacks are an effective means of avoiding most blowouts.

Present technology for preventing blowouts is quite effective. Nevertheless, owing largely to human error and the unpredictability of the drilling environment, some blowouts are inevitable. A recent study evaluating offshore oil production concludes:

> Assuming that present drilling procedures and technologies are used in the future, the rate of serious accidents will probably remain essentially constant with evolutionary improvements in equipment and procedures being balanced by a move into deep water and more hostile environments.[7]

This study also predicts that there will be an average of two major drilling blowouts and two major production accidents each year, assuming maintenance of present OCS production levels.[8] Thus, without a concomitant tightening of safety and equipment standards, an increase in OCS leasing and production rates is likely to result in a proportional increase in major accidents.[9]

Realizing that some large oil spills are inevitable, since the late 1960s the oil industry has been making a major effort to develop a more effective cleanup technology. Containment of the oil slick is the first step in cleaning up a spill. Floating booms placed around the edge of an oil slick are the primary containment devices. A successful containment boom prevents the spreading and thinning of a slick. However, the effectiveness of the booms depends upon such factors as wave height, wind velocity, and currents. Waves in excess of five feet render most booms ineffective.[10]

Besides containment there is the problem of cleanup. Present techniques include the use of mechanical skimmers, absorbents, chemical dispersants, sinking agents, and burning.

Mechanical skimmers remove oil from the water's surface by means of paddle wheels, conveyor belts, or rotational discs. Present skimmers are seriously hampered by heavy seas and have a limited capacity. They are incapable of cleaning up a large-volume, open-sea spill.

Because of its low cost and high absorbency, straw is the most widely used absorbent.[11] Straw is spread upon the spill's surface and then, after it has become saturated with oil, is collected and disposed of. The principal drawbacks of this absorbent is its bulk and disposability. Spreading and harvesting the oil-soaked straw requires considerable manpower.[12] At Santa Barbara, oil-soaked straw had to be trucked 50 miles for disposal.

Chemical dispersants (i.e., detergents or emulsifiers) are sprayed across the surface of the oil slick. Dispersants not only cause the apparent disappearance of the slick, but by breaking it up into large droplets expose more oil surface to bacteria, wind and sun, and thus, theoretically, hasten weathering. Unfortunately, because of their toxicity to marine life, present dispersants are the worst tool for attacking a slick. Heavy use of dispersants led to especially devastating effects on beach and intertidal areas in the aftermath of England's huge *Torrey Canyon* (tanker) spill:

> [D]etergents were being hosed almost continuously, and in high concentrations, onto the surface of the stranded oil, and the milky fluid ran in streams down the shore to the sea. . . . In the exposed middle reaches of the shore, there developed within hours a scene of progressive devastation, and within a few days virtually nothing remained save for tufts of dead and dying algae. The rock surfaces were utterly bare of animals and littered at their bases with cemeteries of shells. Lower down the shore, nearer the low tide mark, the mortality though still great was not total. . . .This was by mid-summer the condition over the greater part of some 150 miles of Cornish coastline.[13]

Because of their toxicity, the use of dispersants in the United States is restricted by federal and state regulations.

Sinking agents such as sand and chalk are spread across the surface of the oil, causing it to sink to the bottom. Unfortunately, spilled oil cannot be swept so easily under the rug—the biologically important bottom sediments are contaminated, and sunken oil tends to rise to the surface at a later time. The United States restricts use of sinking agents to ocean waters exceeding 100 meters in depth where currents are not predominantly onshore.[14] Like chemical dispersants, sinking agents ameliorate the obnoxious appearance of oil pollution without eliminating the pollutant itself.

If it is both fresh and thick, oil on water will burn almost completely. However, in open seas, volatile fractions quickly evaporate, water-in-oil emulsions are formed, and the remaining oil tends to disperse widely in thin films. This makes it nearly impossible to ignite and maintain combustion. Attempts to maintain combustion by adding wicking materials have proved largely futile, primarily because of rapid heat loss to the sea.

To summarize, the environmental arguments surrounding the production of OCS oil hinge on three facts: some large oil spills are inevitable if there is large-scale crude-oil production from the United States Outer Continental Shelf; large oil spills can cause considerable biological and esthetic damage, and present methods for cleaning up large spills are inadequate. These facts support the need for an extensive commitment of resources to preventing large oil spills.[15] (More vigilant regulation and inspection, improved training of production personnel, and tighter specifications of OCS production platforms are the most pressing areas for OCS reform.) However, these facts do not support the inference that, for environmental reasons, the level of anticipated OCS production should be scaled down. Such an inference requires an assessment of the environmental costs of the alternative to higher OCS crude-oil production.

Higher oil imports delivered by tanker are the only feasible substitute for OCS oil over the 1975–85 time span. Because of tanker accidents, the substitution of oil imports for OCS production will not reduce total spillage.[16] Moreover, because tanker accidents are most likely to occur near ports (where shipping lanes are most congested) and because tankers frequently carry refined petroleum products which tend to be both more toxic and less biodegradable than crude oil, these spills tend to be more destructive than equivalent spills of OCS crude oil.

In sum, oil spills are both ecologically and esthetically harmful. However, in most instances, higher OCS production poses fewer environmental hazards than higher oil imports, its only feasible substitute.[17] Hence, there is a positive environmental case for expanding U.S. production of OCS crude oil.

Coal

The United States has enormous coal reserves. Increased coal consumption, especially by electric utilities, is a feasible substitute for imported oil. Unfortunately, increased coal consumption creates two environmental problems: physical disruption of the land caused by mining and emissions of sulphur dioxide and fly-ash particulates from coal combustion.

American coal supplies are divided roughly evenly between the East (Appalachia and the Midwest) and the West (primarily the northern Great Plains). Eastern coal is produced from both underground and strip mines located relatively close to major population centers. Hence, it is cheap to transport. Unfortunately, only 11 percent of Eastern coal reserves can meet present sulphur-emission standards.[18]

Western coal has a low sulphur content. But, because it is located far from major energy-consuming centers and has a relatively low energy content, Western coal is relatively expensive to transport. Present proposals call for this coal either to be shipped directly south, west, and east via unit trains or coal slurry pipelines, or, prior to shipment, to be transformed into electricity or synthetic coal derivatives in giant plants built near the mine mouth.

Because of the relative thickness of known coal seams and the comparatively shallow overburden, nearly all Western coal will be strip mined. The damage due to coal strip mining depends on the geography of the mining site and the magnitude of the reclamation effort.[19] Available water supplies, soil conditions, and the methods used for stripping, storing, and returning the overburden are the key determinants of the success of strip-mine reclamation. The coupling of a high level of rainfall and a reasonably flat terrain makes reclamation fairly feasible in the Midwest.

The northern Great Plains are relatively flat. However, roughly 40 percent of Western coal reserves are in areas receiving an average annual rainfall of less than 10 inches. Reclamation will be nearly impossible in such areas. The other 60 percent of strippable Western coal is found in areas where reclamation will be difficult (hence, expensive) but feasible.

Extensive water supplies are necessary if coal is either burned to produce electricity or converted into synthetic natural gas or crude oil. Indigenous northern Great Plains water supplies are too low to support extensive development of these industries near the mining areas. Hence, most Western coal will have to be shipped directly to the major consuming centers if the Western environment is not to be destroyed.

Electricity generating costs would be lower if Eastern electric utilities were able to burn high-sulphur coal. Before they can do so it is necessary either to relax air-emission standards, to develop an effective and economical coal desulphurization process, or to install devices capable of removing sulphur from air emissions. The Environmental Protection Agency believes that stack gas scrubbers that chemically remove sulphur dioxide from coal emissions are the best way to solve this problem.[20] Many of the nation's largest coal burners (led by American Electric Power) strongly disagree. They point out that the asserted sulphur caused health hazards are unproven, that stack gas scrubbers are expensive, and that the scrubber technology is very complex and, at present, unreliable.[21] Instead of scrubbers, they suggest that coal's sulphur pollution can be effectively controlled by using tall stacks to facilitate wide atmospheric dispersion and by switching to low-sulphur fuels (or even shutting down) during periods when atmospheric sulphur concentrations are judged unacceptably high. These methods of control are of limited value, since they merely disperse the pollutants. Nevertheless, until the stack gas scrubber technology is proven reliable or the more limited methods of controlling sulphur emissions are shown to be inadequate for preventing measurable health hazards, my sympathies in this debate lie with the electric utilities.

Oil Shale

Oil shale—a fine, sedimentary rock which, when heated, yields both oil and gas—is found in abundance in the tri-state area of Colorado, Wyoming, and Utah. The U.S. Geologic Survey estimates that oil shale reserves in the area exceed 600 billion barrels of oil. Unfortunately, most of the United States' extensive oil-shale reserves are located in mountainous, water-short areas. At present, shale oil can be produced commercially only if the shale rock is strip mined and then the oil is removed by heating in huge retorts. Because only a small portion of the shale is actually oil, transportation costs are prohibitive unless retorts are located near the mine. Available water supplies are inadequate, however, to support both large-scale mining and retorting of oil shale. The difficulties of reclaiming strip-mined land in mountainous water-short regions are formidable. "Spent shale," the waste residual that remains after extraction and retorting, presents further difficulties because it occupies some 15 percent more volume than the in-place shale rock. Satisfactory methods of disposing of this sterile, infertile material have yet to be devised. These facts support the conclusion that, at present, large-scale oil-shale production is environmentally unacceptable.

Several companies are presently researching processes for removing oil from shale while it remains underground. Such in situ processes will entail fracturing the shale and remove the oil by either chemical or thermal reactions. The development of a commercial in situ process promises two environmental advantages: There would be no need for strip mining and the refining could be done closer to consuming centers. Large-scale commercial production of shale oil should be delayed for environmental reasons unless a commercial in situ production technology can be developed.

Nuclear Power

Nuclear power generated between 7 and 8 percent of the United States' electricity in mid-1975. Project Independence planners anticipate that the United States' nuclear electricity generating capacity will be quadrupled by 1985. This planned expansion raises three environmental and public safety questions: How safe are nuclear reactors? Can nuclear wastes be safely disposed of? What are the dangers of nuclear theft, proliferation, and blackmail?

The safety record of presently operational commercial nuclear reactors is excellent. There has never been a major release of radioactive materials and no lives have been lost in the few reactor accidents that have occurred. Nevertheless, there is bitter debate over the likelihood of a major reactor accident. The debate centers on the probability of a loss-of-coolant accident and different assessments of the magnitude of the likely damage from such an accident.

If a reactor's nuclear core is not adequately cooled, its nuclear fuel may melt down, breach the walls of the containment vessel, and thereby release radioactive materials into the neighboring environment from which winds and water could disperse deadly amounts of radiation over thousands of square miles. For a loss-of-coolant accident to occur, one of the large pipes carrying cooling water to the reactor core must either rupture or be blocked. In addition, the emergency core-cooling system, which is designed to flood the core with water in the event of a coolant loss, would also have to fail.

Studies commissioned by the Atomic Energy Commission (AEC) have concluded that the probability of a simultaneous failure of both coolant systems is infinitesimal. Thus, press reports of the most extensive AEC-commissioned reactor accident simulation study, by Professor Norman Rasmussen, state that it concludes that there might be one accident per 100 nuclear plants every 2,500 years that would cause 10 or more deaths.[22] Unfortunately, there is contrary empirical and theoretical evidence.

In March 1975, just a few months after release of preliminary drafts of the Rasmussen Report, a fire caused by a careless worker at a nuclear plant owned by the Tennessee Valley Authority (TVA) forced the shutdown of two giant reactors. One reactor was turned off without incident, but the other began to lose coolant and overheat. When that happened, TVA personnel attempted to use the emergency core-cooling system. Because of a power failure caused by the fire, it failed. Fortunately, the operating engineers had time to connect auxiliary pumps by hand in order to flood the core.[23] Nevertheless, this near disaster casts serious doubt on the validity of the Rasmussen conclusions.

The Rasmussen conclusions have also been challenged by other reputable scientists. Most significant, a study team directed by Professor Harold Lewis and jointly sponsored by the AEC and the National Science Foundation issued a report in late April 1975 that concluded: Although the probability of a major accident involving the release of radioactivity seems small, its "quantification (or likelihood) deserves more attention within the reactor safety community than it has received up until now." [24] This study also notes that there is "no comprehensive, thoroughly quantitative" way of evaluating the reliability of the emergency cooling system "because of the inadequacies in the present data base and calculational curves." [25]

The experts also disagree about the damage likely to result from a reactor accident. For example, the Rasmussen Report calculates that the release of radioactivity would cause just 300 deaths from cancer; the Lewis Report estimates that cancer would kill 10,000 to 20,000.[26] An AEC study—kept secret for seven years—calculated that a major accident could kill up to 45,000 people and that "the possible size of such a disaster might be equal to that of the state of Pennsylvania.'' [27]

A second major issue facing the nuclear power industry is the disposal of long-lived and highly toxic nuclear wastes. Can these wastes be sequestered safely from the environment for periods varying from several centuries (for strontium 90 and cesium 137) to a quarter of a million years (for plutonium)? During that period they will have to be protected from both natural disasters like floods and earthquakes and human error or deliberate intrusion. The sad truth is that no one knows whether the technical and institutional capability to insure such isolation exists. [28]

I lack the technical expertise necessary to properly evaluate the environmental and public safety dangers raised by the rapid expansion of nuclear power. Nevertheless, the facts that (1) experts have sharp disagreements about both the probability of a reactor-related nuclear accident and the magnitude of the damage should one occur, and (2) that the problem of permanently disposing of nuclear wastes remains unresolved, prompts me to suggest that our energy policymakers should reduce their advocacy of nuclear power. This suggestion is buttressed by the fact that continued expansion of nuclear electricity generating capacity necessarily increases the possibilities of nuclear theft, proliferation, and blackmail.

Domestic terrorists could threaten the lives of thousands by sabotaging existing nuclear plants. Or, they could acquire enough fuel to build a crude atomic bomb either by stealing small amounts of fissionable material from uranium enriching and reprocessing plants or by hijacking a whole truckload in transit. India's 1974 explosion of an atomic bomb fueled by plutonium taken from a small Canadian-built research reactor demonstrates that any country possessing a nuclear power plant can develop limited nuclear weapons capability. The threat to human life because of nuclear blackmail is presently very real and will be difficult to eliminate.

ENVIRONMENTAL PRIORITIES

Reducing U.S. dependence on insecure oil imports is an important public policy goal. The two surest routes to meeting this goal are to slacken growth in U.S. energy demands and to increase production from domestic sources. Unfortunately, some growth in U.S. energy consumption is unavoidable through at least the early 1980s and higher domestic energy production will have deleterious impacts on the environment, public health, and public safety. These costly impacts may be reduced if most resources are devoted to expanding production from those sources least offensive to the environment.

The production and consumption of natural gas places least stress on the environment: Its combustion is nearly pollution-free and leaked natural gas dissipates quickly and, in most instances, harmlessly into the atmosphere.

Judged by environmental criteria, crude oil is the second best source of domestic energy. Given current production practices, higher output from inland 48 crude-oil sources will cause little additional damage to the environment. Higher production from OCS and northern Alaskan sources will result in some significant environmental damage. However, this should be less than the damage resulting from increasing energy supplies from other sources, including oil imports. Because most undesirable effluents can be eliminated from crude oil during refining, its combustion should not cause significant deterioration of air quality.

Expanded coal production is the third best large-scale alternative. Coal mining does put great stress on the ecology of coal regions and, given current commercial coal emissions control technology, expanded coal combustion will cause a measurable decline in air quality. Nevertheless, I believe that this environmental damage can be held to tolerable levels by judicious siting of new coal mines; by enforcement of strict production, rehabilitation, and safety standards and by enforcement of strict but feasible air emission standards for large coal burners.

Expanded commercial production of nuclear power and oil shale presently pose the greatest danger to the environment and public safety. Prudence dictates a go-slow approach toward nuclear power until the effectiveness of the emergency core-cooling system is demonstrated and explicit measures are taken to reduce the possibilities of nuclear theft and blackmail. Until a commercial in situ recovery process is developed for oil shale, no additional expansion of output is desirable.

CHAPTER FIVE
International Energy Problems

THE WORLDWIDE oil shortages wrought by the OAPEC embargo were over by May 1974. Nevertheless, two fundamental international energy problems continued to plague the oil-importing nations. First, the quintupling of world oil prices since the start of 1973 raised oil importers' costs by about $75 billion annually. As a result, huge quantities of real resources were being transferred to the oil-exporting nations and many importers faced severe difficulties in financing their oil trade. Second, as long as a few large exporters possessed sufficient cohesion to enforce an oil embargo, no nation that was a net oil importer could realistically assume it had guaranteed access to uninterrupted oil supplies.[1]

Because oil demands are very price-inelastic in the short run, quintupled oil prices implied nearly quintupled foreign exchange receipts for OPEC members during 1974. Because the economies of most of these countries were small and/or undeveloped, their ability to consume or invest imported goods and services did not increase nearly as fast as their oil revenues. As a result, OPEC members accumulated a $55 billion current account surplus in their 1974 balance of payments. But, an OPEC trade surplus implies that oil importers suffered an equal trade deficit. Many doubted they would be able to finance such large trade deficits.

Persistent trade deficits are usually financed by long-term loans or direct investments from countries that enjoy trade surpluses. However, most OPEC members were inexperienced in international finance and were averse to making risky investments. Thus, in the panic atmosphere immediately following the oil embargo's onset, it was thought that they would restrict most of their loans to short-term notes issued by the largest banks located in just a few of the most industrialized oil-importing countries.[2] Since these banks were borrowing funds (so-called petrodollars) that might be redeemed at a moment's notice, it was feared that they would be unable to make long-term loans of the necessary magnitude to the less affluent oil-importing countries. This, in turn, might eventually result in the collapse of the international monetary system.

An excellent analysis published by Morgan Guaranty Trust in early 1975 discusses three reasons why such a pessimistic scenario did not and will not occur.[3] First, a post-embargo downward shift in the worldwide demand for OPEC oil and a sharp rise in OPEC members' imports of goods and services caused the annual current account surpluses of the oil-producing countries to peak in late 1974; they began to decline rapidly in 1975. Second, the number of banks receiving OPEC deposits has been growing steadily and petrodollars do not appear to have been concentrated disproportionately in any particular country. Moreover, several deficit countries have received direct loans and grants from OPEC countries—these financed more than a third of the total 1974 oil deficit. Third, loans from existing international banking institutions were sufficient to finance more than half of the 1974 oil deficit. These three reasons suffice to explain why fundamental reforms of the international monetary system were not necessary in order to meet the stresses caused by soaring world oil prices.

Many Americans are concerned because oil exporters (especially Arabs) have used some of their petroleum revenues to buy American businesses. One Senator has been quoted as saying that there is a potential danger in "the use of the control of a United States company in a manner contrary to national security, refusals to supply, dealings with foreign powers . . . the use of a United States company to advance the objectives of a foreign nation." [4] Others fear that Arab-owned American companies may adopt anti-Jewish policies. The United States has the power to negate all such dangers. Existing non-discrimination laws can and should be enforced against any firms that do business in the United States and discriminate against American Jews. Existing laws can also be used to prevent U.S. based firms from taking steps that compromise national security. The United States' experience with German-owned American firms during World

War II (e.g., General Aniline Film) illustrates that in an extreme case foriegn-owned American companies can be nationalized.

The oil-exporting nations reaped tremendous economic and political gains because of the OAPEC embargo. Besides soaring revenues, they were able to force many of the world's most powerful nations to accede to onerous anti-Israeli political demands. The United States will be consuming large quantities of imported oil until at least 1985. The deteriorating economic and political position of the United States as a result of the OAPEC embargo demonstrates that as long as any nation remains a large oil importer it can have guaranteed access to uninterrupted oil supplies only if the large exporters lose their power to enforce an oil embargo. But, an effective oil embargo is possible if, and only if, the major oil exporters possess monopoly power. (This is the case because a monopolist gets his power to set higher than competitive prices from his ability to control output. But, control over output is necessary for an effective embargo. Hence, sellers must have monopoly power if their embargo threats are to be credible.) Therefore, the United States can get lower world oil prices and eliminate the oil-embargo threat prior to 1985 only if the monopoly power of the large oil-exporting countries is destroyed. Accomplishing this result ought to be one of the chief aims of U.S. foreign policy in the post-embargo period.

THE U.S. INTERNATIONAL OIL POLICIES

In an oft-cited, controversial paper published a year before the OAPEC embargo, Professor M. A. Adelman discussed numerous instances in which the State Department advanced a policy of increased cooperation between oil importers and exporters.[5] He concluded prophetically:

> Oil supply is threatened by one and only one danger: a concerted shutdown by the OPEC nations. . . . The cartel is only needed, only exists, to thwart the basic condition of massive potential excess capacity—ability to expand output at costs below prices—and prevent it from becoming actual.
>
> Hence lower prices and secure supply are the two sides of the same coin. . . .

The monopoly may still have its finest hours before it, and prices
should rise well into the decade. . . . The important consuming countries show no sign of understanding their plight. . . . A private monopoly which extracted $1.5 billion per year from consumers would be
denounced and probably destroyed; were they American, some excu-
tives would be in jail. An intergovernmental monopoly ten times as big
is viewed as a bit of redress by the Third World.

What happens to oil in the 1970s depends altogether on the consuming countries. If they are as slow to learn as they have been, then the
projection of $55 billion annual tribute paid the OPEC nations by 1980
may be surpassed.[6]

Repeatedly succumbing to ever-escalating OPEC demands led in-
exorably to the United States' suffering the indignities and high costs
of the OAPEC embargo. Unfortunately, even after the OAPEC embargo conclusively demonstrated the sterility of its "conciliatory" oil
policy, our Chamberlain-like State Department failed to recognize
that neither oil security nor lower prices were likely as long as any
group of large oil exporters possessed monopoly power. In the embargo's immediate aftermath, the State Department chose to ignore
this all-important economic fact and instead pursued a two-pronged
policy aimed at assuaging the oil embargo's ill effects. One element
of this policy was a noisy diplomatic offensive designed to persuade
our OPEC and OAPEC friends, especially the all-powerful Saudi
Arabians, to show their appreciation for the United States' Middle
East peace-making efforts by cutting world oil prices. The second element was to advocate an agreement fixing world oil prices at a
"fair" level. Oil sold for about $1.75 per barrel at the Persian Gulf
in September 1973. In early 1974 the State Department felt that a fair
price was around $6; by December its assessment of a fair price had
apparently risen to more than $8.[7] What price would be judged fair in
future years?

Two instances illustrate the vacuousness of the State Department's
efforts to persuade the Saudis to reward the United States by cutting
prices.[8] On June 8, 1974, a Saudi-American agreement for economic
and military cooperation was announced. The *New York Times* reported that American spokesmen "hoped the new accord . . . would
serve as a model for economic cooperation between Washington and
other Arab nations." [9]

Just two days later the *Times* reported that Saudi Arabia had raised its share of Aramco's revenues—this had the effect of raising the world price of a barrel of crude oil to $9.35.[10]

In mid-October 1974, Secretary of State Kissinger was assured by King Faisal that he would "try to bring down world oil prices." [11] The King repeated this assurance in early November. Apparently, the King's oil ministers were not aware of his statements because the price of Saudi crude oil was raised again in both October and November.[12] As a result of these and other price rises, the price of most Saudi crude oil sold at the Persian Gulf rose from around $7 per barrel at the start of 1974 to $10.36 per barrel by year-end. Cynical Americans could only hope that the State Department would discontinue this diplomatic offensive.

The State Department's efforts to promote a worldwide oil-price agreement were equally ill advised. Events since 1970 conclusively demonstrate that the OPEC countries adhered to price agreements only so long as they were in their interests. For example, the Tehran agreements made in early 1971 to guarantee stable and predictable prices for a five-year period were revised within six months. Subsequent revisions occurred with increasing rapidity. Whenever circumstances made higher prices possible, one of the OPEC countries "reluctantly" initiated price hikes. The other members immediately followed. Hence, price agreements have been a worthless tool for holding down OPEC's oil prices. There is no reason to suspect that price agreements will not be as worthless in the future. Even worse, they are likely to entail two very high costs. First, as long as the oil cartel remains strong, the agreed-upon price will offer a minimum target level to charge. Within a few months of any price agreement, OPEC militants can be expected to advance persuasive arguments explaining why even higher prices are justified. If OPEC has sufficient unexploited monopoly power, further price hikes will soon follow. Second, since the oil-importing countries tend to have considerably higher regard for the sanctity of economic contracts than their OPEC suppliers, a worldwide price agreement would tend to fix a solid floor for oil prices, even though OPEC's monopoly power might be eroding. The probability that the agreed-upon price will become a sturdy floor becomes even more likely in view of the fact that, following the embargo, the State Department asserted that high world oil prices were desirable because they would facilitate the development of alternative high-cost domestic energy supplies.

Soaring surplus productive capacity was putting pressure on the OPEC cartel in early 1975. World oil prices were finally beginning to fall. Chapter 6 explains why, as time passes, these supply pressures can only grow. Establishing a worldwide crude-oil price can only help OPEC to sustain its monopoly power by thwarting these oversupply pressures. Because anything that helps OPEC to maintain its monopoly power hurts vital security interests of the United States and its Western European and Japanese allies, the State Department's proposed worldwide oil-price agreement was foolhardy.

The State Department's other post-embargo international energy policy initiatives have not been as undesirable as the two discussed above. For instance, the Department correctly realized that increased cooperation between the major oil-consuming nations could help both to reduce the probability of another embargo and to alleviate the ill effects should one nevertheless occur. To foster increased cooperation, the Department took the lead in establishing the International Energy Agency (IEA)—an organization composed of 16 major industrial nations as of year-end 1974, but not including France. Even before IEA's first formal meeting, its members had agreed to a plan for cutting back consumption and sharing oil supplies in the event of another embargo. Plans to establish a multibillion-dollar lending facility for IEA members suffering from severe balance-of-payments difficulties were also well advanced. In an attempt to offset the indirect support that the lending facility would give to oil prices by providing financing for continued high levels of imports, the State Department proposed the borrowers must demonstrate that they were taking effective steps to reduce their oil-import demands.

Because the problems of recycling petrodollars had been exaggerated, the IEA's new lending facility was probably unnecessary. Also, the IEA quickly became a moribund international agency. Nevertheless, taken in toto, these policies to facilitate cooperation among the major oil importers ought to have had the desired results of reducing slightly their vulnerability to sudden supply interruptions and chipping away at OPEC's monopoly power.

Accommodating OAPEC and OPEC demands was the misguided

strategy underlying the United States' major post-embargo international energy policy initiatives. However, the United States also implemented three measures that were manifestations of an alternative and preferable confrontation strategy. First was the decision by Congress—over the objections of Secretary of State Kissinger—to add a clause to the Trade Act of 1974 denying trade preferences to any developing country that:

> . . . is a member of the Organization of Petroleum Exporting Countries, or a party to any other arrangement of foreign countries, and such country participates in any action . . . the effect of which is to withhold supplies of vital commodity resources from international trade or to raise the price of such commodities to an unreasonable level and to cause serious disruption of the world economy.[13]

This clause was of little immediate practical consequence. In the mid-1970s most OPEC members were exporting inconsequential quantities of other commodities to the United States. However, because many OPEC countries (e.g., Iran, Saudi Arabia, and Venezuela) plan to devote a large fraction of their oil revenues to developing energy-intensive export industries such as aluminum, petrochemicals, and steel, its importance could rise in the future. Thus, OPEC members were correct when they inferred that this clause was hostile to their future interests. As would be expected, evidence of opposition to OPEC demands by the United States triggered a hostile, but largely vocal, OPEC reaction. It did not precipitate either further price hikes or another embargo and it has had the desirable result of helping to dissuade others (e.g., Mexico) from joining OPEC or similar commodity cartels.[14]

A second modest anti-OPEC policy initiative emanated from a surprising source, Secretary of State Kissinger. In January 1975, he responded to the question, "Have you considered military action on oil?" with the statement:

> . . . I am not saying that there is no circumstance where we would not use force. But it is one thing to use it in the case of a dispute over price, it's another where there's some actual strangulation of the industrialized world.[15]

Later in the same interview, the Secretary added a disclaimer:

. . . I want to make clear, however, that the use of force would be
considered only in the gravest emergency.[16]

The Secretary's highly qualified statement caused an uproar among
oil exporters. Charges of "Yankee imperialism" came from all the
usual sources. Nevertheless, an official statement indicating that the
United States might be forced to respond with force if there were
another oil embargo was long overdue. Sudden embargoes of key
productive resources threaten vital economic interests of all importing
countries. Hence, they can only be regarded as warlike acts, whether
they are motivated by economic, military, or political considerations.
The oil-exporting nations deserved to be informed that repetitions of
the embargo tactic could precipitate strong military countermeasures
by the United States.

The third and most important anti-OPEC measure was President
Ford's decision to place a tariff on oil imports in order to discourage
their consumption. The tariff was to begin at $1 per barrel on Febru-
ary 1, 1975, and was to rise to $2 on March 1 and $3 on April 1. The
President labeled the tariff an interim measure—he hoped Congress
would replace it with a comprehensive excise tax of $2 per barrel on
all oil sold in the United States. In an attempt to arrive at a compromise energy policy with Congress, he delayed imposition of the second installment until June 1 and, the third installment was never imposed. Nevertheless, raising the cost of insecure oil imports is
desirable. The chief flaw with the Ford tariff is its failure to make any
allowance for the fact that the United States suffers different security
risks depending on the source of its oil imports. For example, oil imports from Arab countries are demonstrably more likely to be interrupted than oil imports from other countries. A way of circumventing
this shortcoming is outlined in the following discussion of alternate
policy options.

OTHER POLICY OPTIONS

Until OPEC's monopoly power is in large part destroyed, vital security interests of the United States will be endangered. In view of
this threat, other foreign policy options aimed at eroding OPEC's mo-

nopoly power merit serious consideration. One option that attracted widespread support from both Congressional Democrats and the media in early 1975 was M. A. Adelman's suggestion that the United States impose a quota limiting oil imports to an acceptable level and then sell the import rights by sealed competitive bids.[17] The principal benefits claimed for this policy are that it could be used to gradually reduce U.S. dependence on imported oil and to encourage increased competition among oil exporters wishing to sell in the huge American market. Specifically, since the productive capacity of the world oil industry far exceeds current demands and since most "surplus" oil would cost less than 50 cents per barrel to produce, huge potential profits await any exporter who can sell more oil at or near current world prices. Thus, nearly all exporters would be eager to sell more oil at current prices in the American market. But, assuming an oil-import quota is adopted, the amount of oil that any exporter can sell in the United States is limited to the number of import rights it possesses. These rights would be purchased initially at an auction in which both the identity of the bidders and the amounts would be secret. In view of the huge profits awaiting any nation that can sell more oil to the United States, each would have a strong incentive to cut prices indirectly by raising the amount it bids for these import rights. If this happens, even higher bids (hence, sharper price cuts) are likely to be submitted at subsequent sales of import rights by those disgruntled bidders who bid too low at the earlier sale.

Adoption of an Adelman-type quota proposal holds considerable promise for facilitating the erosion of the oil cartel's monopoly power and would be preferable to the conciliatory policy actually being pursued by the United States. However, it is subject to at least four criticisms. First, because the OPEC countries will realize that the intent of this policy is to promote their cartel's disintegration, it is quite likely that they will agree simply to refrain from bidding for the U.S. import rights. After all, these countries are conservative investors who have never before been "charged" for the privilege of selling their valuable oil. If OPEC members do react in this manner then the most likely purchasers of the import rights would be oil companies who would offer to pay a very low price for the import privilege. Having won this right, they would, presumably, go shopping for oil from the world's major exporters. The incentive for these countries to offer price concessions would be no stronger than it has been in the absence of a quota.

Second, if they feel sufficiently provoked, the OPEC countries might decide to challenge the U.S. anti-OPEC policy by announcing new reductions in output and higher prices. The United States would then be faced with the distasteful choice of either capitulating to these demands or of escalating the confrontation.

Third, as outlined above, the oil-import quota proposal takes no account of the fact that the United States suffers different security risks depending on the source of its oil imports. Professor Adelman suggests that the import quota could be modified to take account of this factor by offering partial refunds to nations that had never threatened embargo. Some such modification would be desirable. Unfortunately, it would be nearly impossible to do this and also preserve a bidding system that is really secret.

Fourth, suppose the United States does adopt oil-import quotas again. Past experience suggests that they will continue to be enforced long after the OPEC threat disappears. Oil-import quotas were abolished by Presidential executive order in 1973 because the

> . . . Mandatory Oil Import Program . . . has the very real potential of aggravating our supply problems, and it denies us the flexibility we need to deal quickly and efficiently with our import requirements. General dissatisfaction with the program and the apparent need for change has led to uncertainty. Under these conditions there can be little long-range investment planning for new drilling and refinery construction.[18]

It would be unfortunate if the United States had to repeat its costly experience with oil-import quotas in the mid-1980s.

The oil-import quota proposal is aimed at causing a gradual reduction in United States' dependence on insecure oil imports and encouraging increased competition among OPEC members. An alternative policy that should have similar desirable results and is less likely to be subject to the four criticisms just discussed would be for the United States to impose a high tariff on all oil imports and then negotiate (or unilaterally grant) partial or total exemptions for imports from countries that satisfy specific security criteria.[19] For example, countries exporting oil could be divided initially into three classes. Secure countries might include those whose borders are contiguous to the United States and have never been OPEC members (currently both Canada and Mexico)—oil imports from these countries should be charged zero tariff. Insecure countries could include all countries that joined in the OAPEC embargo (all Arab oil-exporting countries except Iraq)—oil imports from these countries might be charged a $5 per barrel tariff. Oil imports from all other countries would be charged a $2.50 per barrel tariff. A differential tariff appears to be no more difficult than the quota to administer. In addition, it should have three desirable results.[20] First, it would reduce U.S. oil imports and encourage a sharp shift in their composition away from insecure sources. Second, it would foster jealousy between those OPEC members who have been given different tariff classifications. In a time of surplus capacity this should damage the cohesion that presently binds the cartel members together. Third, it would offer strong inducements both for suppliers of secure oil to attempt to expand current output and for other suppliers to offer guarantees sufficient to persuade the United States to reclassify them into a more favorable lower tariff category. Conversely, those nations that continued to take steps that threatened the security of American oil supplies would do so knowing that they would be reclassified into a higher tariff category.

CONCLUSION

The State Department has failed to recognize that destruction of the oil exporters' monopoly power is both the necessary and sufficient condition for reestablishing U.S. oil security prior to the mid-1980s. Even after the OAPEC embargo most of the State Department's policies continued to be aimed at reaching accommodation with the oil exporters. If recent history has any lesson to teach us, it is that policies of this type are doomed to failure.

CHAPTER SIX

The Future of OPEC

THE WORLDWIDE HAVOC and energy price explosion wrought by the OAPEC embargo of oil sales established the large oil-exporting nations who dominate the OPEC cartel as a key force shaping international events in the mid-1970s. Because OPEC oil has no substitutes available at short notice and large quantities of new non-petroleum energy will be available no earlier than the mid-1980s in most industrialized countries, it is easy to predict that OPEC will play a leading role in shaping the substance of international economic relations for a long time to come. After examining economic, political, and technological factors likely to affect the performance of world petroleum markets over the next ten to fifteen years, the ultimate aim of this chapter is to describe what OPEC's future role is likely to be.

THE PETROLEUM PRODUCTION PROCESS

The sum of exploration, development, and operating costs measures the total resource costs that must be incurred when producing crude oil or natural gas. Exploration costs are paid to the productive factors, such as labor and capital, used to search for new oil and gas reserves in areas where their presence is suspected but unsure. Development costs pay for constructing the facilities necessary to produce previously discovered petroleum reserves. Operating costs are incurred when existing production facilities are run so that crude oil and natural gas may actually be extracted from their natural sources. These three types of resource costs are unavoidable if new petroleum reserves are to be found and produced.

This chapter borrows extensively from Richard B. Mancke, "The Future of OPEC," *Journal of Business*, 48 (1) (January 1975): 11–19.

Enormous geological variations distinguish oil and gas fields in different parts of the world. Because Persian Gulf oil fields tend to be unusually large, numerous, and productive, the total costs necessary to find, develop, and produce the typical new barrel of this oil were estimated to be less than 20 cents in the late 1960s.[1] In sharp contrast, much of the new oil that must be produced in the United States—if the goals of Project Independence are to be realized—will come from small, scattered, low-productivity fields.[2] The total resource costs of large amounts of this oil will be greater than $8 per barrel.[3]

Besides explaining huge regional differences in the costs necessary to produce crude oil, regional differences in the likely size, incidence, and productivity of petroleum sources also explain why there are corresponding differences in the speed with which previously unplanned expansions in a region's crude oil output can take place. Specifically, because huge but largely undeveloped reserves of low-cost crude oil have already been discovered in such Persian Gulf countries as Iran, Kuwait, and Saudi Arabia, their output can be expanded sharply merely by drilling the necessary additional wells and installing the appropriate surface gathering and storage facilities. Because of the size and accessibility of these Persian Gulf oil fields, there is only about a one-year lag between a decision to raise planned future output from these sources and the date when significant quantities of that new output can come on stream.[4] In contrast, specific locations of large hitherto undeveloped but commercial oil fields are simply unknown in most non–Persian Gulf oil-producing countries. Hence, large amounts of additional exploration are a necessary prerequisite for a large expansion of new oil supplies from these areas. Completion of this exploration will usually take several years. In addition, because newly discovered oil fields in these areas will usually be much smaller, less productive, and less accessible than new Persian Gulf fields, the time needed to develop them commercially is necessarily longer. For these reasons, the minimum lag between a decision to raise future crude-oil output appreciably above presently planned levels and the date when large amounts of this output will first come on stream is presently three to six years in areas like the U.S. Gulf of Mexico or the British North Sea and up to ten years in frontier areas such as the Alaskan North Slope or northwestern Canada.

In sum, because of unavoidable exploration and development lags, changes in the previously planned rate of growth of a region's oil production act as if they obey the laws of inertia. Specifically, for a long time there is no visible payoff from steps taken to expand oil output above previously planned levels. Then, only after most exploration has been completed and extensive development of the newly discovered oil fields has begun, the first dribbles of commercial production appear. As time passes and development of the new field is nearly complete, these dribbles grow into a far larger stream. At this stage, relatively little additional effort is required to keep the supply of "new" oil flowing unabated for several years.

REASONS FOR OPEC'S POST-1970 SUCCESSES

The OPEC cartel was formed in 1960 in order to stop falling world oil prices. Nevertheless, because the growth of new oil supplies exceeded the growth of demand, world oil prices trended downward throughout the 1960s.[5] OPEC had failed to achieve its proclaimed goal. The price actually paid for a barrel of crude oil at the Persian Gulf fell from about $1.50 in 1960 to between $1.10 and $1.20 in early 1970; but by late 1975 it had soared to more than $11. Why did the 25-year trend of falling postwar world oil prices end in 1970? Why did world oil prices explode upward during the next five years? The chief reasons for this sudden turnabout were misguided policies of acquiescence by the major oil-importing countries (especially the United States; see chapter 5) and a dramatic change in the underlying supply conditions of the world oil market that greatly strengthened OPEC's bargaining power.[6]

Daily non-Communist crude-oil output rose more than 8.3 million barrels over the three years between 1967 and 1970. Table 6.1 lists twelve countries that contributed significantly to this rise.[7] The four largest contributors were Libya, Iran, Saudi Arabia, and the United States.

The year 1970 marked a transition in the world oil industry. In part because already developed petroleum sources were being depleted

Table 6.1
Changes in Output by the Major Oil-Producing Nations

| | 1967–1970 | | 1970–1973 | |
| | Absolute Change (thousand barrels per day) | Percent of Total Non-Communist Change [a] | Absolute Change (thousand barrels per day) | Percent of Total Non-Communist Change [a] |
Nation				
Libya	1,641	19.7	-1,198	-14.2
Venezuela	148	1.8	- 326	- 3.9
U.S.A.	696	8.3	- 318	- 3.8
Saudi Arabia	840	10.1	4,170	49.3
Iran	1,157	13.9	2,108	24.9
Nigeria	681	8.2	1,053	12.4
Abu Dhabi	NA		657	7.8
Canada	315	3.8	521	6.2
Indonesia	355	4.3	463	5.5
Iraq	290	3.5	446	5.3
Kuwait	451	5.4	280	3.3
Algeria	168	2.0	86	1.0
Total Non-Communist World	8,342	100.0	8,461	100.0

Source: American Petroleum Institute, *Petroleum Facts and Figures* (Washington: American Petroleum Institute, 1971); and *The Oil and Gas Journal,* December 28, 1970 and February 25, 1974.

[a] Entries in this column do not sum to 100% because production by several small countries is excluded.

faster than new supplies were being discovered and developed, production in three of the most important crude-oil producing countries—Libya, the United States, and Venezuela—hit its all-time peak. Table 6.1 shows that between 1970 and 1973 daily crude-oil output in these three countries actually fell by slightly more than 1.8 million barrels. But over the same three-year period, insatiable world crude-oil demands grew another 8.5 million barrels daily.

Because of declining output in Libya, the United States, and Venezuela, rising world oil demands could be sated only if other countries lifted their daily production rates by slightly more than 10 million barrels between 1970 and 1973. Because delays are unavoidable when crude-oil output is to be boosted above previously planned levels, only Iran and Saudi Arabia, with their already known huge, low-cost reserves, were in a position to expand production quickly enough to fill the gap. Thus, Table 6.1 shows that between 1970 and 1973 Saudi Arabia provided nearly 50 percent of the 8.5-million-barrel rise in the non-Communist world's daily crude-oil output; Iran added another 25 percent.

In sum, in the years immediately preceding 1970 many countries, even including the United States, were competing to supply the non-Communist world's growing crude oil demands. No one country, or small group of countries, played a dominant role. In contrast, during the early 1970s only two countries—Iran and Saudi Arabia—supplied nearly three-fourths of the net additions to world oil demands. Given their dominant position as oil exporters, a decision by either of these countries to cut back production would have led to severe shortages in world oil markets. This dramatic change in the underlying economic structure of the world oil industry appreciably enhanced the monopoly power of Iran and Saudi Arabia and of OPEC—the organization that these two countries increasingly came to dominate. Various OPEC members chose to exercise their new power by threatening to embargo oil sales unless their customers paid higher prices or agreed to take anti-Israeli political stands. Because of Iran's and, especially, Saudi Arabia's ever-tightening control over incremental world oil supplies, these embargo threats became increasingly credible after 1970. As a result, oil consumers capitulated and world oil prices began to escalate rapidly.

NEW PETROLEUM SUPPLIES IN THE LATE 1970s

The huge Prudhoe Bay oil field was discovered in 1967; subsequently significant oil and natural gas deposits were found in northwestern Canada. In 1970, the first of many large crude-oil discoveries was made in the North Sea; also, the United States government increased its sales of oil land leases on the Outer Continental Shelf. Because the lag between discovery and initial production of oil from any of these new sources is several years, none yielded appreciable flows of crude oil prior to 1975. This state of affairs will change rapidly in the second half of the 1970s.

The North Sea will be the world's most important new oil theater through at least 1985. In the five years following the first large North Sea discovery more than 30 commercial fields were found. Seven were designated "giants" (i.e., recoverable reserves greater than one billion barrels). Some idea of the magnitude of the North Sea oil play may be inferred from a comparison with Texas, where daily crude-oil production averaged roughly 3.6 million barrels in 1973. Over a period spanning more than 50 years of intensive exploration, only four giant Texas fields have been discovered. The rash of large discoveries of North Sea oil in the first half of the 1970s virtually guarantees that several additional North Sea fields will be honored with the "giant" designation prior to 1980.

The first really large quantities of North Sea oil began to be shipped via pipeline from Norway's Ekofisk field to Teesside, England, in early 1975. Daily Ekofisk shipments rose quickly to 300,000 barrels by mid-year. Commercial quantities of crude oil were also found in six other distinct fields in the Ekofisk vicinity prior to 1974. Development of most of these fields is already well advanced. Production is expected to begin coming on stream in 1976. With the addition of this oil, the pipeline connecting Ekofisk to Teesside should be shipping oil at its nearly 1-million-barrel planned daily capacity before 1980.

Large quantities of oil will begin flowing from several British North Sea fields during 1976–77. British Petroleum's exploration manager has estimated that daily shipments from Britain's North Sea waters will reach 500,000 barrels by the end of 1976.[8] Daily shipments from just three British giants—Brent, Forties, and Ninian—are expected to total about 1.5 million barrels in 1980.[9] At least another 1 million barrels can be expected from smaller British fields that will be in advanced stages of development by late 1975. Moreover, because the oil companies are now geared up for a major North Sea oil play, additional large quantities of North Sea oil can be expected to be coming on stream by 1980 from fields that will be discovered prior to 1977. To summarize, if 1974–75 development plans are merely carried out, daily crude-oil production from British and Norwegian North Sea waters will total at least 3.5 million barrels in 1980; in addition, the North Sea will be the source of a large addition to Western Europe's natural-gas supplies. However, if the British and Norwegian governments encourage new exploration and development, daily output of as much as 6 million barrels of North Sea oil seems possible by the early 1980s.

Alaska's huge Prudhoe Bay field has recoverable crude-oil reserves of at least 9.6 billion barrels. This should yield a daily output of nearly 2 million barrels when fully developed.[10] It was initially expected that delivery of Prudhoe Bay oil would begin in late 1972. However, because of delays resulting from environmental review procedures, construction of the pipeline necessary for delivering this oil was not even authorized until late 1973. When work on the trans-Alaskan pipeline finally began in early 1974, its owners expected that daily shipments of about 1.2 million barrels would begin in mid-1977; these were expected to be built up to around 2 million barrels by 1980.[11] Experience with North Sea petroleum pipeline construction estimates suggests that some slippage is likely in the trans-Alaskan pipeline's construction schedule. Nevertheless, barring an unforseeable interruption, Americans will certainly be consuming large quantities of Prudhoe Bay oil well before 1980.

American oil companies began extensive offshore operations in the late 1940s. During 1975 about 1.5 million barrels of crude oil per day came from OCS sources. The United States held relatively few large offshore lease sales between 1962 and 1970. Resumption of large-scale offshore leasing began in December 1970, when more than a half million acres were leased for $846 million. This was followed by eight lease sales from 1972 through 1974 in which roughly $10.5 billion was paid for rights to produce oil and natural gas from slightly more than 3.5 million acres. Because the time lag from lease sale to significant production is three to six years in U.S. OCS waters, most of the offshore oil produced in the United States during the mid-1970s came from federal lands leased prior to 1962. Oil companies will not say how much oil they expect to produce from recently leased offshore lands. However, if they are to recover their mammoth $11-plus billion 1970–74 OCS leasing investments, these lands will have to provide well over 1 million barrels per day of crude oil or natural-gas equivalents by 1980.[12]

The United States established four Naval Petroleum Reserves between 1912 and 1924 to provide fuel for the Navy's wartime use. Naval Petroleum Reservation Number 1 at Elk Hills, California, has 700 million barrels of proved reserves—only trivial amounts of its oil have ever been produced. Responding to a request by President Ford, Congress has been considering legislation authorizing the production and sale of up to 350,000 barrels of crude oil daily from Elk Hills. Elk Hills is likely to be producing 170,000 barrels within one year of the passage of this legislation; daily output could rise to 300,000 barrels a year later.

Exxon's Santa Ynez field, located in California's Santa Barbara Channel, has estimated reserves of 1.3 billion barrels, making it one of the five largest oil fields in the United States. Development of this giant field was halted following the 1969 Santa Barbara spill. Exxon was allowed to resume development of Santa Ynez's oil reserves only in 1974. It expects Santa Ynez to produce 30,000 barrels per day by 1978 and around 80,000 barrels daily by the early 1980s.[13]

The consummation of exploration and development plans that were already underway in the years prior to the OAPEC embargo virtually guarantees that additions to new oil supplies from the North Sea, northern Alaska, and the U.S. OCS will total at least 6 million barrels daily by 1980. In addition, the quadrupling of oil prices during 1973–74 has triggered a surge of petroleum exploration and development throughout economically less developed parts of the world. Because of post-embargo discoveries, several less developed countries that are not OPEC members (e.g., China, Malaysia, and Mexico) could anticipate in 1975 that they would become large net oil exporters by the early 1980s. Besides triggering an accelerated search for petroleum reserves, higher prices were a key factor causing a sudden end to the annual 5+ percent growth rate in worldwide postwar oil consumption. World oil consumption actually fell between 1973 and 1975. It is likely to resume rising as the major industrial countries pull out of the 1974–1975 recession. However, as long as world crude-oil prices (deflated) stay near their high 1974 levels, the growth in consumption will remain far below pre-embargo levels. To summarize, as a result of the twin phenomena of a sharp fall in the rate of growth of world oil consumption and a large increase in non-OPEC petroleum supplies, world oil markets are beginning to undergo a second dramatic change: Before the end of this decade OPEC members will begin to face vigorous competition for the privilege of satisfying world oil demands from a small collection of industrialized Western countries; by the early 1980s, a larger collection of less developed countries will also be joining in the competitive fray.

LIKELY TRENDS IN FUTURE WORLD OIL PRICES

As non-OPEC oil production begins its inexorable sharp rise, world oil markets will witness another major structural change. What does this mean for OPEC? Or for the industrialized oil-consuming nations? The two scenarios outlined below are intended to bound the range of possible conditions in world oil markets during the late 1970s.

Throughout the 1960s crude oil was cheaper than most other fuels (except natural gas). After the OAPEC embargo this was no longer true—oil had become more expensive than both coal and nuclear power. Given both ample time and the persistence of 1974 real prices on world markets, OPEC oil has many politically secure substitutes. Repetitions of embargo threats guarantee that the major oil-consuming countries will begin to develop these substitutes and take steps (e.g., tighter import quotas, higher tariffs, and higher excise taxes) designed to cause further sharp reductions in their consumption of OPEC oil; also a severe embargo could precipitate direct military intervention. Having already achieved both high prices and vast political power, OPEC would be foolish to provoke such a response. Thus, even if OPEC's monopoly power were to remain undiminished in the late 1970s, it is unlikely that its members would take measures causing world oil prices to rise above 1974 real levels.

At the other extreme from maintaining something like the very lucrative late-1974 status quo, it is possible that each OPEC member's desire to raise its share of the total oil profits will cause an outbreak of competition for increased sales and, as a corollary, send world oil prices tumbling. Assuming a total breakdown of the OPEC cartel, oil prices at the Persian Gulf could actually fall far below 1970 levels.

Neither of the boundary possibilities just discussed seems likely to occur in the second half of the 1970s. On the one hand, because of sharply higher oil prices and worldwide recession, demand for OPEC oil began falling in 1974. This trend should continue as large new crude-oil and natural-gas supplies from the North Sea, northern Alaska, and offshore United States commence.

Faced with sharply falling sales and revenues, several OPEC members (e.g., Abu Dhabi, Ecuador, Indonesia, Libya, and Nigeria) actually cut their price slightly in early 1975. Nevertheless, at a September meeting OPEC members agreed to raise their oil prices by 10 percent. The price of Saudi Arabian light crude—the marker crude for OPEC oil pricing—was raised by this amount. However, most other oil exporters did not raise their prices proportionately. Hence, the average rise in world oil prices after OPEC's September meeting was only about 7 percent. Because world prices of other (i.e., non-oil) industrial goods and agricultural commodities rose at an average annual rate of more than 20 percent during the first nine months of 1975, the deflated world price of oil has fallen below the late 1974 peak. As the decade progresses OPEC members will have to enforce increasingly severe production cutbacks if they are to prevent additional cuts in real prices. Cartels usually find that it is difficult both to arrive at and to enforce agreements aimed at cutting back production from previously planned levels. On the other hand, Saudi Arabia and (to a lesser extent) Iran will continue to be OPEC's dominant members throughout the 1970s. Their market shares will remain large enough so that either can always retard or even halt falling world oil prices by unilaterally cutting back exports. If oil prices begin falling too quickly it will be in their interest to do so in order to prevent an even costlier outcome—OPEC's disintegration.

The prognosis for OPEC's future becomes much bleaker in the early 1980s. By then, new output due to the sharply higher post-embargo levels of petroleum exploration and development will be coming on stream in a large number of less developed countries. These countries will wish to sell at lucrative world prices all the oil they can produce in excess of their usually small domestic needs. Unless the larger oil-importing countries choose to support policies fixing world oil prices, a sharp fall in oil's real price appears likely at this time.

A DANGER

Chapter 5 explained why any erosion of OPEC's monopoly power will advance economic, political, and security interests of the major oil-importing countries. Hence, it is in their interest to adopt policies that encourage erosion of OPEC's monopoly power and thus lower world oil prices. Unfortunately, there are two reasons for suspecting that contrary policies may instead be pursued. First, several countries have made national commitments to achieve energy independence. By itself this should reduce demand for OPEC oil. However, to achieve energy independence, some countries may take steps to guarantee high domestic fuel prices. The rancorous oil-import quota debate in the United States throughout the 1960s demonstrates that it is often politically difficult for governments to maintain high domestic prices for a product that sells for far less on world markets. To circumvent this domestic problem, the governments of several important oil-consuming nations may be prompted to support policies for maintaining high world oil prices. Second, when energy prices are high, those owning low-cost domestic supplies can reap high rents from their sale.[14] The recipients of these rents will mount a strong fight to maintain them by urging adoption of a national policy to forestall energy price cuts. The United States' past experience with oil-import quotas, market-demand prorationing, and the oil-depletion allowance suggests that the rent recipients may once again prove to be successful.[15] If they are, the cost to consuming countries may be the adoption of policies that foster high world oil prices and thus, indirectly, promote OPEC's monopoly.

CHAPTER SEVEN
Competition in the Oil Industry

IN THE DISMAL first months following the OAPEC embargo, a variety of widely quoted opinion makers—including elected and appointed public officials, consumerists, editorial writers, and even some Persian Gulf potentates—were quick to resurrect a familiar charge: that U.S. petroleum problems were caused primarily by the monopolistic abuses of the giant integrated oil companies. Americans' implicit belief in the validity of this charge provided the rationale for at least two post-embargo policies aimed at limiting "Big Oil's" economic power and at redistributing its "ill-gotten" gains. First, following a Congressional directive, the Federal Energy Administration issued regulations designed to enforce those integrated oil companies that were both large and had above-industry-average domestic crude-oil supplies to share these low-cost supplies with their less fortunate (and, arguably, less capable) crude-short competitors.[1] Second, Congress chose to exempt small crude oil producers when it passed tax legislation eliminating the infamous oil depletion allowance in early 1975.[2] Perhaps of greater future importance, belief in the validity of the monopoly charge provides the principal rationale for those advocating the establishment of a federal energy company to engage in one or more areas of the oil business.

Large, vertically integrated companies participate in all facets of the oil business: They produce and sell crude oil from domestic and, frequently, foreign sources; they transport crude oil from the wellhead to refineries and ship finished oil products to retailers, and they produce and sell a great variety of refined products and petrochemicals. Have the large integrated oil companies succeeded in monopolizing one or more of these markets? To answer this question it is necessary to examine three types of economic evidence:

1. Whether the market structure is more conducive to competition or monopoly. Generally those markets that contain many strong competitors and are easily entered by new competitors are thought to be the most competitive.
2. Whether the firms doing business in the relevant market engage in conduct (e.g., pricing, product, or legal tactics) that facilitates collusive behavior.
3. Whether most of the firms in the industry earn persistent and otherwise inexplicable high profit rates.

THE EVIDENCE: MARKET STRUCTURE AND CONDUCT IN THE MAJOR FACETS OF THE PETROLEUM INDUSTRY

Whenever a product's price exceeds the cost of producing an additional unit, producers will find it profitable to produce and sell that unit. Unfortunately for them, if each producer follows what he perceives to be his self-interest and produces all units for which price exceeds cost, industry output will expand, causing prices to fall and profits to dwindle. The price fall will stop only when the profit incentive to expand output ceases. This level of output will be reached only when price equals the total costs of producing additional units.

The process just described is called competition. Realizing that the ultimate result of competition is lower profits for every firm in the industry, producers of almost any product desire to avoid it. To do so each must act to limit its sales. However, each will do so only if it has good reason to expect that its competitors will do likewise. Monopoly power is being exercised when the members of an industry are successful in reducing their output and thereby keeping their product's price higher than the cost of producing additional units. Monopoly power is likely to be stronger the fewer the number of firms presently in or potentially able to quickly enter an industry, the easier collusion is, and the less aggressive the industry's customers are when searching for lower-priced alternatives.

The Sherman Act provides the foundation for most of the United States' federal antitrust policies. Its two famous substantive provisions are Section 1, which prohibits contracts, combinations, and conspiracies in restraint of trade, and Section 2, which prohibits monopolization, attempts to monopolize, and combinations or conspiracies to monopolize. Section 1 focuses on the defendants' market conduct. A firm will be found guilty of violating Section 1 if the plaintiff can prove that the firm has engaged in anti-competitive agreements (e.g., price fixing) with other firms in the industry. Section 2 focuses

Table 7.1
Sherman Act Section 2 Precedents Compared

I. Major Cases Finding Defendant to Violate Section 2				
Case	Entry	Number/Strength of Competitors	Reasons for Success	Defendant's Market Share
Alcoa (1945)	None	No domestic competition	Patent monopoly, cartels and preemption of raw materials	80–90% of industry for 25 years
United Shoe (1953)	Only one significant entrant	No significant competitors	Merger, acquisition, discriminatory 10-year leases	85% of market for 40 years
American Tobacco (1946)	None in 8 years	Several small competitors	Conspiracy to fix prices and exclude competitors	75% of cigarette market for 40 years, declining slowly
Grinnell (1966)	None effective	No significant competitors	Mergers and agreements not to compete	87–91% of market

II. Major Cases Finding Defendant Not to Violate Section 2				
Case	Entry	Number/Strength of Competitors	Reasons for Success	Defendant's Market Share
du Pont (1956)	Substantial	Many in flexible wrappings; only 2 in cellophane	Competitive achievement and willingness to take risks	75% of cellophane, 20% of flexible wrappings
Hughes Tool (1954)	Some successful entrants	Four significant competitors	Best product and excellent service	75% of roller bit industry and stable for 20 years

Source: Cravath, Swaine, and Moore, *Pretrial Brief for International Business Machines* (submitted to the U.S. District Court Southern District of New York, January 15, 1975), pp. 4–5.

on the structure of the market which the firm is alleged to monopolize. In order to prove a Section 2 violation it is usually necessary to demonstrate that the market structure is conducive to monopolizing acts. Table 7.1 summarizes the key market structure parameters in the major Section 2 cases. Special notice should be given to the fact that each of the firms found guilty of violating Section 2 accounted for 75 + percent of the relevant product market, had few large competitors, and experienced little or no entry by competitors into its market.

Foreign Crude Oil

The price of nearly all of the crude oil sold by the OPEC countries in early 1975 was ten to a hundred times greater than its total resource cost.[3] Because, relative to current and projected levels of demand, the OPEC countries have huge quantities of low-cost oil reserves, the persistence of price-cost differentials of this magnitude offers conclusive proof that the OPEC countries are monopolistic sellers of crude oil.[4] Chapters 5 and 6 have argued that the two keys to OPEC's monopoly power in the mid-1970s have been the ability of its most important members to implicitly agree to production cutbacks and the relative acquiescence to OPEC demands by the principal oil-importing countries. Do the international oil companies also exercise monopoly power in the market for foreign crude oil?

Available evidence on both the structure of the world crude-oil market and the conduct of the international oil companies supports the judgment that, in the years prior to OPEC's formation in 1960, the major international oil companies enjoyed significant but eroding monopoly power.[5]

Prior to the mid-1950s virtually all of the oil traded internationally was produced by the subsidiaries of eight companies: British Petroleum (BP), Compagnie Française des Petroles (CFP), Exxon, Gulf, Mobil, Royal Dutch Shell, Standard Oil of California (Socal), and Texaco. In the Middle East these companies were joint participants in a variety of crude-oil-producing and marketing consortia. Moreover, encouraged by the American, British, and French governments, the charters of these consortia included restrictions severely restricting competition between the eight. Two examples will suffice to illustrate this point.

1. American oil companies first entered the Middle East by acquiring a share in the Iraq Petroleum Company from BP, CFP, and Shell. "The price of establishing the first American presence in the Middle East was the 1928 Red Line Agreement which obligated the consortium members not to compete against each other within the area of the old Ottoman Empire." [6] Exxon and Mobil—which acquired the entire American interest in the Iraq Petroleum Company in the early 1930s—were subject to the anticompetitive strictures of the Red Line Agreement until 1974.

2. In 1933 Socal obtained an exclusive 60-year oil concession in Saudi Arabia. Desiring both additional financing and marketing facilities, Socal took in Texaco as an equal partner and formed a new subsidiary named Caltex. Caltex's Aramco subsidiary discovered enormous low-cost crude-oil reserves in Saudi Arabia. The appearance of this oil on the world market following the conclusion of World War II threatened the market power of the five established international majors—BP, CFP, Exxon, Mobil, and Shell. The prospects for Exxon and Mobil, whose only Middle East oil came from their jointly held minority interest in the Iraq Petroleum Company, were especially bleak. Both firms needed more oil to supply their Western European affiliates but they were prevented from acquiring new Middle East sources by the Red Line Agreement. Hence, they feared that "Caltex . . . would be able to use Aramco to build up a marketing organization no other firm could compete against. Exxon and Mobil therefore decided to offer their markets and their capital to Caltex in return for a piece of Aramco." [7] After considerable negotiation Caltex accepted the Exxon-Mobil offer.

   Broadening Aramco's ownership to include two companies that had access to other sources of crude oil, both within and outside the Middle East, seriously reduced the competitive impact of Saudi oil. Aramco, when solely owned by Caltex, had sold its oil at cost (which was far below the prevailing world price) to Socal and Texaco. Both companies then reaped high profits when refined products made from it were sold in Western European markets. Having access to lower-cost crude oil, the Caltex partners were offering severe price competition in refined-products markets that had traditionally been dominated by the other international majors. Shortly after Exxon and Mobil assumed partial ownership of Aramco, they persuaded Caltex into agreeing that Aramco should be transformed into a profit-maximizing entity that sold oil to its owners at the world price. The net result of this change was to eliminate the special incentive for Socal and Texaco to expand refined-products sales and thus to reduce competition in world oil markets.

Beginning in the mid-1950s several companies (both American and foreign) joined the eight majors in producing Middle Eastern crude oil. Because the most promising Persian Gulf oil concessions were under the nearly exclusive ownership of the eight majors, the new competition was initially on a very small scale. This was not the case in Libya. Not wanting to be controlled by any single economic entity, that country's 1955 Petroleum Law established a fragmented pattern of oil concessions. Many American companies with no significant foreign oil reserves acquired Libyan concessions. By the early 1960s several of these companies had discovered and developed large oil reserves. Libyan developments, coupled with rising European sales of Soviet crude oil and natural gas, resulted in a rapid increase in the level of competition between firms that produced and sold crude oil on world markets. By the early 1970s scores of producing companies were significant participants in the world petroleum market. Also, as the OPEC members gained power and successfully demanded that they be given partial ownership over their oil, the number of effective restrictive agreements between the eight international majors dwindled rapidly.

Because of sharp changes in both the structure of the world petroleum market and in the conduct of the industry's firms, the available evidence no longer supports the inference that the large international oil companies continue to exercise significant monopoly power in the world crude-oil market. Hence, it is fatuous to blame present and near-future international energy problems on the monopolistic practices of these companies. As Professor M. A. Adelman told a Senate committee in January 1975:

Sheik Yamani and his colleagues knew that the oil companies are in the public doghouse, and that millions of people will call a price hike a reduction if you can only make the companies out as villains. The public attitude toward the multinational oil companies brings me back to the bad old days of Joe McCarthy. Then, many of our people, frustrated, angry, and a bit fearful of the unreachable leaders of the "monolithic Communist bloc," went out determined to find and bash an enemy at home. Today, unable to do anything about high oil prices, many of our citizens are inclined to take it out on the multinational oil companies. But these companies are simply obeying the United States government, which has made them into instruments of the cartel, and our government can take those functions away from the companies and leave them to the work of providing the oil.[8]

Domestic Crude Oil

Compared with most other major natural-resource-based industries (e.g., aluminum, copper, and steel) the American crude-oil industry is not highly concentrated. Table 7.2 shows that as of 1969–70 the industry's largest firm accounted for less than 10 percent of all American production. Moreover, thousands of very small firms compete successfully in this industry. The role played by small companies is especially crucial in the vital exploration phase. In 1974 small companies (defined as not in the largest thirty) drilled 86.2 percent of all exploratory wells.[9] The chief reason for the large number and vitality of small companies is the absence of significant-scale economies in producing crude oil from onshore inland 48 sources. Hence, new entry into this industry is easy. Professor James McKie has described the most common ways firms enter the crude-oil industry:

> Many oil-producing companies originated as successful wildcat enterprises. While a few firms may begin with a large supply of capital and immediately undertake an extensive drilling program, the typical firm got its start through a series of fortunate single ventures, often involving exploratory deals with established major or independent firms. New corporations and partnerships are frequently budded from the existing ones. . . . A geologist or petroleum engineer may gain enough experience on his own, making good use of the associations he has built up in the industry. . . . An employee of a drilling contractor may work up from platform hand to superintendent. Once known to purchasers of drilling services and sellers of equipment, he finds it relatively easy to set up his own firm. . . . After operating as a contract driller for some time, he may be willing to put one of his rigs into a wildcat venture on a speculative basis. . . . In this way drilling contractors frequently become independent producers. . . .
>
> Another way to enter oil and gas exploration is via brokerage. Exploration enterprise swarms with middlemen anxious to arrange produc-

ing deals. . . . A speculative broker may arrange a prospecting deal
among other parties . . . and usually retains for himself a small interest in the venture. Since technical training and apprenticeship are not
strictly necessary, this route is crowded with hopeful shoestring pro-
moters along with the experienced entrepreneurs.[10]

The twin facts that the domestic crude-oil industry embraces tens
of thousands of viable firms and that new entry continues to be easy
strongly support the inference that the economic structure of this
market is effectively competitive. However, one caveat is necessary.
To produce crude oil from either the Alaskan North Slope or the
Outer Continental Shelf presently requires an initial investment totaling millions of dollars. The importance of oil supplies from these two
frontier areas will grow rapidly over the next several years. While the
growing importance of crude oil from frontier sources will make it increasingly difficult for small, one-man companies to enter the business, it seems unlikely to seriously diminish effective competition.
Presently, the 19 large oil companies listed in Table 7.2 are all active
participants in one or both of the United States' promising frontier oil
regions. Many smaller oil companies are also active in these areas. In
addition, many large industrial companies and public utilities (e.g.,
Bethlehem Steel, Peoples Gas, Reynolds Industries, and the Union
Pacific Railroad) have also invested large sums in search of frontier
oil. I suspect that no other large American industry enjoys the participation of so many large wealthy firms.

When an industry has many firms and entry is easy, collusive behavior becomes nearly impossible unless all of the industry's major
firms are tied together by explicit price-fixing and market-sharing
agreements. Such agreements would violate Section 1 of the Sherman
Act. There is no evidence that they exist in the American crude-oil
industry. Without collusive agreements, monopoly prices can usually
be charged only if the government enforces anticompetitive policies.
As chapter 1 explained, enforcement of market demand prorationing
by the major oil-producing states and oil-import quotas by the U.S.
government did raise the price of American crude oil far above competitive levels throughout the 1950s and 1960s. However, import
quotas have been abolished and, largely as a result of the worsening
shortage of domestic oil, prorationing presently has little real effect.

Table 7.2
Company Shares of Domestic Net Crude Oil
Production and Proved Domestic Crude Oil Reserves
(in percent)

Company	Share of Domestic Production (in 1969)	Share of Domestic Proved Reserves (in 1970)
Exxon U.S.A.	9.76	9.92
Texaco	8.47	9.31
Gulf	6.78	8.97
Shell	6.08	5.98
Socal	5.31	8.97
ARCO	5.11	7.48
Standard (Ind.)	5.09	8.46
Mobil	3.94	4.87
Getty	3.38	3.85
Union	2.88	3.18
Sun	2.47	2.67
Continental	2.21	2.77
Marathon	1.64	2.37
Phillips	1.55	3.55
Cities Service	1.28	2.49
Amerada Hess	1.04	2.49
Tenneco	0.99	0.90
Skelly	0.88	1.09
Superior	0.74	1.03
Top 4	31.09	37.17
Top 8	50.54	63.88

Source: U.S. Federal Trade Commission, *Preliminary Federal Trade Commission Staff Report on Its Investigation of the Petroleum Industry* (June 1973), Tables II-1 and II-2.

In sum, available market structure and industry-conduct evidence supports the inference that in the mid-1970s the market for American-produced crude oil is effectively competitive.

Transportation

Crude-oil products are the most versatile and readily transportable major type of energy. Hence, they tend to be consumed far away from the wellhead and therefore transportation is a key stage in the oil business. All of U.S. imports of crude oil and refined products, with the exception of those from Canada, are shipped via tanker. Within the United States approximately 75 percent of crude and 27 percent of products is carried by pipeline; the remainder is carried by tankers, barges, and trucks.[11]

Oil companies own as much as one-third of non-U.S. private tanker capacity. The remaining capacity is chartered, either under short-term (spot) contracts or long-term contracts averaging five years duration. Economists who have studied the tanker market agree that it is one of the most competitive in the world.[12] M. A. Adelman has written:

> Each individual ship available for spot charter is, in effect, like a separate firm and the worldwide market allows no protected enclaves. . . . In any given month, several dozen ships are offered for oil company use all over the world by several hundred owners, none with over 5 percent of total tonnage. Tacit collusion would be impossible, and no attempt at open collusion has been made since World War II. . . . [The] ''spot'' charter market therefore seems purely competitive.
>
> This time-charter market is linked to the spot market at one end, and at the other to the cost of creating new capacity. Here entry is open and cheap. . . . Moreover, there are no strong economies of scale in ship operations. Many owners have only one ship. . . . But to say that many competent firms cluster on the boundaries of the industry, and that minimum capital requirements are low, is to say that entry is easy and market control impossible.
>
> With many ships available in the short-run, and easy entry for the long-run what possibility is left for control in the meantime? Little if any in theory, and none can be observed in practice. Tankship owners, oil companies and independents cannot control the long-term supply even in concert, for anyone contemplating a production or refining investment and needing the transport services has time to charter a ship or buy a new one.[13]

Since the 1973–74 oil embargo, there has been a new trend in the world tanker market: many OAPEC countries have begun to acquire tanker fleets. Already the charge is being made that OAPEC tankers pose a new threat to the security of oil importers because they may refuse to deliver oil. Since the trend to increased OAPEC tanker ownership seems likely to continue, this charge will be heard with increasing frequency. It should be ignored. The oil-exporting countries will have monopoly power as long as they can act together to limit crude-oil sales. Their control over access to crude-oil production already gives them this power. Hence, even if they could monopolize the tanker market (and for the reasons discussed above this is unlikely) it would not enhance their total monopoly power.

The United States is traversed by an extensive network of crude-oil and refined-petroleum-product pipelines. Gathering lines collect crude oil from wells and transport it to larger-diameter main trunklines that go to one or more refineries. Product pipelines carry gasoline and other products from the refinery to local or regional storage facilities. Because large pipelines are expensive to build, most are owned directly by individual major oil companies or by several majors participating in joint ventures.[14] Because of the physical fact that a cylinder's volume (hence throughput) increases proportionately faster than its circumference (hence capital costs), pipelines enjoy extensive-scale economies; i.e., larger pipelines have lower unit costs. The twin facts that the pipeline business is relatively concentrated and that pipelines enjoy extensive-scale economies suggest that established pipeline companies may face little competition.[15] In part for these reasons, interstate pipelines come under the "common carrier" regulatory jurisdiction of the Interstate Commerce Commission.

The Interstate Commerce Commission (ICC) has the responsibility for insuring that the interstate pipelines do not discriminate against nonowners. It attempts to do this by regulating rates and assuring that all shippers are granted access. Nevertheless, many nonowners charge that the ICC has been derelict in performing this duty. They maintain that a variety of business practices have been used to deny them access to common carrier lines. These alleged practices include requiring unnecessarily large minimum-size shipments, granting nonowners irregular shipping dates, limiting available storage at the pipeline terminal, and imposing unreasonable product standards upon pipeline customers.[16] If true, such charges are serious. Therefore they ought to be investigated. However, since the ICC already possesses regulatory authority, no additional legislation is required.

Refining

The oil-refining industry transforms crude oil into more useful finished petroleum products. Table 7.3 lists the principal products of U.S. refineries—gasoline accounts for nearly 50 percent of the total. As of January 1, 1974, the United States had 132 oil-refining companies; 17 had a daily capacity in excess of 200,000 barrels.[17] Table 7.4 lists the share of domestic gasoline-refining capacity of the twenty largest companies in 1970. The largest, Exxon U.S.A., accounted for less than 10 percent of the total. Compared with other major American heavy industries, oil refining is not highly concentrated.

Table 7.3
Principal Products of U.S. Refineries
in 1969

Product	Percent
Gasoline	45.5
Distillate fuel oil	21.6
Jet fuel	8.2
Residual fuel oil	6.8
Kerosene	2.6
Lubricants	1.7

Source: U.S. Federal Trade Commission, *Preliminary Federal Trade Commission Staff Report on Its Investigation of the Petroleum Industry* (1973), p. 18.

Depending on their complexity and size, new oil refineries cost between $50 and $500 million. Many, including the Federal Trade Commission (FTC), infer that such high capital requirements constitute a significant barrier to new entry. Events immediately following the elimination of oil-import quotas in May, 1973, fail to support this inference. As Professor Leonard Weiss has testified (in his role as an expert witness for the Antitrust Division of the Justice Department in *United States* v. *I.B.M.*):

I mentioned . . . the number of firms, including some independents I have never heard of, who set out to build refineries between May and

Table 7.4
Top Twenty Companies Share of U.S. Gasoline
Refining Capacity, 1970

Company	Share (percent)
Exxon U.S.A.	9.22
Texaco	9.19
Standard (Ind.)	7.94
Shell	7.69
Socal	6.72
Gulf	6.47
Mobil	6.30
ARCO	6.25
Sun	4.54
Phillips	4.24
Union	3.24
SOHIO	3.09
Cities Service	2.26
Ashland	2.11
Continental	2.03
Marathon	1.92
Getty	1.76
Tenneco	1.35
Clark	1.21
American Petrofina	0.85

Source: U.S. Federal Trade Commission, *Preliminary Federal Trade Commission Staff Report On Its Investigation of the Petroleum Industry* (1973), Table II-3.

July of 1973, and it is just astounding—and these were one hundred million dollars and many one hundred million dollar investments—that shook my belief in capital requirement as a high barrier to entry quite a bit.[18]

Because of the OAPEC embargo and the resulting sharp fall in projections of future United States petroleum demands, many of these plans to build new refineries were subsequently canceled. Nevertheless, as of year-end 1974, 11 companies were still planning to complete new U.S. refineries in the mid-1970s. They are listed in Table 7.5. The diversity of these firms does not support the contention that large firms in the American refining industry enjoy the protection of high entry barriers.[19]

Table 7.5
New U.S. Refining Capacity Set for 1975–77

Company	Date Set	Location	Added Capacity (barrels/day)
Exxon U.S.A.	1976	Baytown, Tex.	250,000
	1975	Baton Rouge, La.	14,000
	1975	Bayway, N.J.	30,000
ECOL Ltd.	1976	Garyville, La.	200,000
Socal	1975	Perth Amboy, N.J.	80,000
	1975	Pascaguola, Miss.	40,000
	1976	Richmond, Cal.	175,000
	1976	El Segunda, Cal.	175,000
Dow	1977	Freeport, Tex.	100,000
ARCO	1976	Houston, Tex.	95,000
Champlin	1976	Corpus Christi, Tex.	60,000
Clark	1975	Hartford, Ill.	45,000
Vickers	1975	Ardmore, Okla.	30,000
Texaco	1977	Lockport, Ill.	25,000
Douglas Oil	1975	Paramount, Cal.	15,000
Energy Co. of Alaska	1977	Fairbanks, Alaska	15,000

Source: Leo R. Aalund, "Inflation and Uncertainty Cut U.S. Refining Buildup," Oil and Gas Journal (November 25, 1974), p. 37.

Marketing

Marketing is done by jobbers who purchase refined oil products and supply retail dealers. Many jobbers are completely independent of refiners and dealers; others own their own retail outlets; and still others are simply marketing extensions of the oil refiners. Also jobbers may carry branded or unbranded products. Table 7.6 presents national gasoline market shares of the leading 25 marketers in 1973. After examining similar evidence, the Federal Trade Commission concluded: ". . . gasoline marketing is the most competitive area of the petroleum industry and has the largest number of independent companies." [20] Lacking evidence of collusive conduct in regional or local markets, I concur.

Table 7.6
Share of National Gasoline Market, 1973

Company	Percent of U.S. Market
Texaco	7.97
Exxon U.S.A.	7.64
Shell	7.47
Standard (Ind.)	6.90
Gulf	6.75
Mobil	6.49
Socal	4.78
ARCO	4.37
Phillips	3.92
Sun	3.67
Union	3.05
Continental	2.30
Cities Service	1.66
Marathon	1.52
Ashland	1.48
Clark	1.25
SOHIO	1.23
Hess	1.00
BP	0.81
Tenneco	0.78
Murphy	0.66
Getty	0.65
American Petrofina	0.63
Skelly	0.60
Triangle	0.57

Source: Harold Wilson, "Exxon and Shell Score Gasoline Gains," *Oil and Gas Journal* (June 3, 1974), p. 78. Cites results of the Lundberg Society.

THE EVIDENCE: OIL COMPANY PROFITABILITY

Available evidence on market structure and conduct supports the unpopular conclusion that the American oil industry is more competitive than most other comparable large American industries. Available evidence, summarized below, on the oil industry's profitability also supports this conclusion.

Total Profitability

One test of the successful exercise of monopoly power is the persistence of abnormally high industry profits over a long period of
time. Judged by the most common measure—the after-tax rate of return on equity investments—profits of American oil companies were
below the average for all American industrial firms for the ten years
prior to 1973.[21] Largely as a result of shortage-caused higher prices,
oil company profits rose sharply during 1973–74. However, they
began to fall off in the last quarter of 1974 and this trend accelerated
in 1975. The fact that unusually high profits were earned for a period
of less than two years that coincided with a period of unanticipated
supply shortages is not evidence of monopoly.

Accounting profitability measures are only loosely related to the
economist's profit definition. Professor Edward Mitchell has described several problems plaguing the accounting data:

> Expenditures that should be capitalized, such as advertising and re-
> search and development, frequently are not. Depreciation charges
> usually reflect simple arithmetic rules rather than actual changes in the
> value of assets. Future income not yet confirmed by sales contracts is
> ignored. Even without these problems, the procedure of estimating the
> rate of return on capital by the ratio of income to stockholders' equity
> . . . can give widely disparate answers for a given true rate of return
> depending upon the particular time pattern of cash flows.[22]

In an attempt to circumvent the problems with accounting data,
Mitchell calculated the profits actually realized by owners of oil company common stocks. Specifically, he calculated the total stockholder
profits by taking the price of a company's stock at a beginning point
in time, assuming all dividends were immediately reinvested back
into the firm, and then calculating the value of the initial and acquired
stock at the ending time point.[23] Table 7.7 reprints Mitchell's calculations of the average annual rates of return realized by oil company
stockholders over two periods, 1953–72 and 1960–72. Based on this
data Mitchell concluded:

1. American petroleum companies were significantly less profitable
   than the S & P (Standard and Poor's) 500 over the 1953 to 1972

period. Indeed, not one of the twenty-one American petroleum companies equaled the S & P 500's rate of return!

2. The eight companies charged by the Federal Trade Commission with monopolizing the industry earned an average rate of return of 12.1 percent, more than 20 percent below the S & P norm for the 1953 to 1972 period.

3. From 1960 to 1972 domestic producers realized less than half the rate of return of the S & P 500.[24]

Table 7.7
Oil Industry Stockholders' Average Annual Rate
of Return * and Standard and Poor's 500 Stock
Composite Index, 1953–72 and 1960–72
(in percent)

Refiners	1953–1972	1960–1972	Producers	1953–1972	1960–1972
Domestic			*Domestic*		
American Petrofina	—	18.5	Aztec	—	8.9
Ashland	13.8	13.6	Baruch-Foster	—	0.9
Atlantic Richfield	12.8	14.6	Consolidated	—	4.9
Cities Service	10.5	9.7	Crestmont	—	−4.8
Clark	—	19.0	Crystal	—	4.8
Commonwealth	—	11.8	Felmont	—	8.7
Continental	9.0	6.9	General American	8.9	11.5
Crown	—	9.0	Louisiana Land	—	13.7
Getty	12.3	16.0	Superior	9.0	8.9
Husky	—	11.4	Westates	—	5.5
Kerr-McGee	14.6	18.3	Average	9.0	6.3
Marathon	9.7	10.2			
Murphy	—	10.5	*Canadian*		
Phillips	9.4	7.8	Canadian Export	—	6.4
Reserve	—	−5.2	Canadian Homestead	—	24.9
Shell	9.9	6.8	Canadian Superior	—	14.3
Skelly	10.2	12.5	Dome	21.4	32.0
Standard (Ind.)	11.7	15.3	Home	—	15.8
Standard (Ohio)	15.4	16.1	United Canso	—	20.3
Sun	7.1	9.4	Average	21.4	19.0
Union	11.1	12.8			
			Overseas		
Average	11.3	11.7	Asamera	—	37.5

Table 7.7 (*Continued*)

Refiners	1953–1972	1960–1972	Producers	1953–1972	1960–1972
International			Belco	—	4.7
Exxon	11.6	10.7	Creole	—	5.2
Gulf	12.3	8.9	Occidental	—	23.8
Mobil	13.3	15.3	Average	—	17.8
Standard (Cal.)	11.4	10.2			
Texaco	13.7	9.7			
Average	12.5	11.0			
Canadian					
Gulf Oil of Canada	—	11.1			
Imperial Oil	12.4	17.2			
Pacific Petroleum	—	12.3			
Average	12.4	13.5			

Standard and Poor's 500 Stock Composite Index
1953–72   15.6
1960–72   12.8

Source: Edward J. Mitchell, *U.S. Energy Policy: A Primer* (Washington: American Enterprise Institute, 1974), Table B-1.

* Annual rate of return that would yield same increase in value over the period as realized price appreciation with dividends reinvested. Figures shown are averages of three rates of return based on three alternative price assumptions: (1) Stock purchased at initial year's high, sold at final year's high, with all dividends reinvested at succeeding year's high, (2) stock purchased at initial year's low, sold at final year's low, with dividends reinvested at succeeding year's low, and (3) stock purchased at initial year's closing price, sold at final year's closing price, with dividends reinvested at succeeding year's closing price.

The rather poor profit performances realized by these major oil companies is inconsistent with the charge that they were exercising substantial monopoly power.

Profitability of Offshore Oil Investments

Because of the relatively much higher costs of lease acquisition and production, fewer firms are actively involved in producing off-shore oil. Moreover, offshore oil is frequently produced by joint ventures of several oil companies. For these reasons, monopoly returns seem especially likely to be realized in this sub-business. Nevertheless, a rather large number of economic studies have failed to find any evidence of monopoly.[25] For example, a U.S. Bureau of Mines study concluded that the typical successful offshore tract in the Gulf of Mexico yielded a return on total assets of between 14 and 17 percent—many tracts are unsuccessful.[26] And Professors Edward Erickson and Robert Spann concluded, after examining the process of leasing offshore lands, that "oil and gas companies earn no more than a competitive rate of return on offshore drilling." [27]

THE EVIDENCE: SPECIAL MONOPOLY ARGUMENTS

When judged by the conventional market structure, industry conduct, and industry performance criteria, the conclusion that the American oil industry is relatively competitive is unavoidable. Hence, proponents of the thesis that the American oil industry is monopolized have had to develop a special monopoly argument.[28] As outlined by the Federal Trade Commission: ". . . the major oil companies in general and the eight largest majors in particular have engaged in conduct . . . squeez[ing] independents at both the refining and marketing levels." [29] This ability to squeeze "has its origin in the structural peculiarities of the petroleum industry" which allow the majors to "limit effectively the supply of crude oil to a point which reduces refinery profits to zero. Clearly, such a system creates a hazardous existence for independent refiners who have little or no crude production." [30]

Squeezing could be both profitable and successful only if the integrated majors enjoyed special advantages over their independent competitors. The Federal Trade Commission mistakenly argued that they enjoyed two, import quotas—which were abolished in 1973—and the oil depletion allowance—abolished for large oil companies in 1975:

1. The import quota clearly contributed to profits earned in producing crude oil by elevating prices, but the quota increased profits to the major in another way. The right to import went only to existing refineries. Thus the major companies . . . were able to purchase oil at the world price as an input for their refineries, which produced final products at elevated domestic prices. . . .[31]

2. Oil depletion allowances [allowed] . . . a crude oil producing firm
   . . . to subtract from its gross income before taxes an amount equal
   to 22 percent of its total revenues from crude production. . . .
   Under this system the major integrated firms have an incentive to
   seek high crude prices. The high crude prices are, however, a cost
   to the major firms' refineries. Thus, an increase in crude prices
   implies an increase in crude profits but a decrease in refinery profits.
   The integrated oil companies gain because the depletion allowance
   reduces the tax on crude profits, while refinery profits are not subject to the same advantageous depletion allowance.[32]

The arguments just summarized are fallacious.

Under the Mandatory Oil Import Quota Program the general rule
for allocating the valuable oil-import rights was that they be given to
domestic refiners as a percentage of their total crude-oil inputs. However, the allocation formula was a sliding scale that granted small
refiners a far larger proportion of imports. Table 7.8 calculates the
value in 1969 of the per barrel subsidy which the sliding scale
awarded three refiners of very different size. The small refiner received a per barrel subsidy more than five times higher than the largest. This result was not atypical. But, this means that the FTC was
wrong when it stated that the allocation of oil-import rights provided
the large integrated majors with a tool for squeezing their smaller independent competitors.

The FTC's second charge was that, because the oil depletion allowance reduced the effective tax rate on crude-oil profits, the large
integrated majors raised the price of crude oil and thereby diverted
taxable profits from refining operations to crude-oil operations. As a
result, the FTC continued, independent refiners were squeezed. Although sounding plausible, this charge was flawed since, using the
FTC's own data, 16 of the 17 largest integrated majors would have
found profit-shifting unprofitable.

The FTC's analysis was wrong because it failed to take proper account of the fact that most of the integrated majors were not self-sufficient in crude oil. To operate their American refineries at desired
levels they had to buy crude oil from independent domestic producers. On the assumption that the oil depletion allowance was 22

Table 7.8
Per Barrel Subsidies Awarded to Three
Oil Refiners in 1969 *

Firm	1 Daily Total Crude Oil Input [a]	2 Daily Total Crude Oil Imports Allowed by Sliding Scale	3 Gross Value of Daily Import Rights [b]	4 Per Barrel Subsidy to Refiner [c]
Standard (N.J.)	992,000 barrels	35,810 barrels	$53,715	5.41¢
Clark	97,651 barrels	8,886 barrels	$13,329	13.65¢
Husky	11,000 barrels	2,060 barrels	$ 3,090	28.09¢

Source: Richard Mancke, *The Failure of U.S. Energy Policy* (New York: Columbia University Press, 1974), Table 7-4.

* These calculations are intended to be illustrative only. They are premised on two simplifying assumptions: 1) The refineries of all three firms are located in Districts I-IV; 2) None of these firms was claiming "historical" import rights.

[a] Estimates of daily crude oil inputs are obtained from Moody's. These are approximations.

[b] The right to import one barrel of oil into Districts I-IV was worth about $1.50 in 1969 (see *The Oil Import Question*). Thus the product of $1.50 times the daily crude oil imports allowed yields the gross value of import rights.

[c] Obtained by dividing column 3 by column 1.

percent, profit-shifting would only yield higher profits for those companies able to produce at least 93 percent of their crude oil needs.[33] Table 7.9 reproduces the FTC's estimates of crude oil self sufficiency for the 17 largest integrated American refiners in 1969. Except for Getty Oil, only the sixteenth largest, none of these integrated giants produced more than 93 percent of its total domestic needs. Hence, none enjoyed enough crude-oil self-sufficiency for profit-shifting to be profitable. The after-tax losses because any of these firms adopted this strategy would have ranged from a low of 3 cents on each dollar of profits shifted by relatively oil-rich Marathon to a high of 48.3 cents on each dollar of profits shifted by relatively oil-poor Standard Oil of Ohio.[34] None of these 16 integrated majors would choose to bear these high costs. This implies that profit-shifting was never practiced, and thus, that independent refiners were not being squeezed.

Table 7.9
The FTC's Estimates of the
Domestic Self-sufficiency of 17 Leading
Refiners in 1969

Company	Self Sufficiency (percent) of runs to stills)
Standard (N.J.)	87.4
Standard (Ind.)	50.5 [a]
Texaco	81.0 [b]
Shell	62.1
Standard (Cal.)	68.8 [a]
Mobil	42.2 [c]
Gulf	87.6 [a,d]
ARCO	64.9
Sun	46.7 [e]
Union	64.3 [a]
Standard (Ohio)	6.7 [a]
Phillips	51.8 [a]
Ashland [f]	12.6
Continental	64.0
Cities Service	49.9
Getty [g]	137.2 [d]
Marathon	88.1

Source: Preliminary Federal Trade Commission Staff Report on Its Investigation of the Petroleum Industry (July 1973), p. 20.

[a] Other liquids included in crude production.

[b] Estimated.

[c] Other liquids included in refinery runs.

[d] Excludes crude processed for company's account.

[e] Crude production includes Canada.

[f] 12 months to September 30, 1969.

[g] Includes subsidiaries.

SUMMARY OF THE EVIDENCE

Four significant factual conclusions were established in the preceding discussion:

1. Many firms (both large and small) participate in each stage of the oil business and entry appears to be relatively easy.

2. There is no evidence that oil companies are presently engaged in wide-ranging collusive practices.
3. Oil companies have not enjoyed abnormally high profits that have persisted over a long period of time.
4. The special "squeezing" arguments are implausible because adoption of the hypothesized tactics would have cost the large oil companies (i.e., the alleged squeezers) billions of dollars annually to implement.

This evidence is inconsistent with charges that the giant American oil companies are exercising significant monopoly power. A well-designed U.S. energy policy will be possible only when both the public and the government admit that our energy problems are not due to the machinations of a few giant oil companies.

FEDERAL OIL AND GAS COMPANIES

Since the OAPEC embargo there have been many Congressional proposals to establish a federal oil and gas company that would participate in one or more phases of the petroleum business. Senator Adlai Stevenson summarized the principal rationale behind most of these proposals when he stated that Americans can no longer "afford to turn sole responsibility for [the] price and supply of natural gas and oil over to the very same companies which have already used the gasoline shortage they helped to create to drive their competition out of business. . . ." [35] The fact that this rationale is false casts serious doubt upon the wisdom of all policies premised upon it. Nevertheless, since these proposals are becoming increasingly popular, they merit more detailed criticism.

The Stevenson Proposal

On November 7, 1973, Senator Stevenson introduced legislation to create a Federal Oil and Gas Company (FOGCO). [36] He proposed granting FOGCO extensive powers:

The Corporation would have access to publicly owned gas and oil rights on Federal lands, as well as the power to acquire similar rights on private lands. It could enter into the full range of activities necessary for the exploration, development, refining, transportation and marketing of the petroleum and gas products. However, it would be able to enter into activities outside exploration, development and production only if it were unable to sell its crude oil and natural gas to companies which would promote competition in the industry.

The Corporation would have the authority to issue bonds to cover its indebtedness, and Federal appropriations in the amount of $50 million per year would be authorized for the first ten years.[37]

And he defined the purpose of this legislation as being

. . . not . . . to provide a forerunner for nationalizing the American petroleum industry. The purpose is to develop public resources—and preserve the free enterprise system in the petroleum industry. But private oil companies need a spur, a yardstick, an incentive and competition. This Corporation would provide that yardstick.[38]

Proponents of FOGCO argue that it is not a precursor to nationalization of the petroleum industry but rather an attempt to stimulate competition. Whatever the announced intention, there can be no doubt that creation of a FOGCO-type public energy company would represent a fundamental change in relations between the U.S. government and the oil industry. Before legislating such a dramatic change it would be prudent for Congress to make a serious effort to answer the following questions:

1. Is the rationale for FOGO legitimate?
2. Will creation of FOGCO discourage large amounts of new private investments in the petroleum business?
3. Is FOGCO likely to operate as efficiently as private firms?

What are the likely answers to these questions?

Besides being premised on the false assumption that the American petroleum industry is monopolized, the FOGCO proposal also mistakenly assumes that its creation ". . . would give the Nation a 'yardstick' against which to judge the performance of the private oil companies." [39] The chairman of the board of Standard Oil of Indiana was correct when he told the Senate Commerce Committee that:

. . . the major fallacy in this use of the "yardstick" concept is that a yardstick is employed to measure similar entities. With no taxes to pay, no leases to purchase, no stockholders to reward, and the choice of government acreage on which to operate, customary business measurements would be completely lacking in the case of a Federal Oil and Gas Corporation. Any so-called "yardstick" thus established would be totally artificial and without meaning.[40]

The legislation establishing FOGCO does grant it several competitive advantages. Industry spokesmen feel (perhaps correctly) that this can only discourage new private investment. Thus, the president of the American Petroleum Institute (the chief trade association of the industry) has testified:

> Soothing words may be uttered that there is no intention of nationalizing or socializing the petroleum industry. But will potential investors be convinced? What would you think if you were a potential investor in a private enterprise company that would be placed in competition with a government-owned company with all its unique advantages? [41]

Finally, there is reason to suspect that a government company may be less efficient than its private counterparts. Some FOGCO critics arrive at this conclusion by pointing to the present problems of two widely criticized public enterprises: Amtrak and the United States Postal Service. This analogy is probably inappropriate—at their creation both of these public concerns were saddled with an obsolete physical plant and the responsibility for providing numerous money-losing services. Presumably FOGCO would not be so encumbered. Much more serious is the prospect that FOGCO's management is likely to discover that it must consider the political ramifications of what should be merely business decisions. This is likely to create severe administrative problems in a business that is already risky and requires high levels of technical expertise. For example, will FOGCO's management feel free to risk hundreds of millions of dollars on necessary wildcat exploration when its performance is being monitored continuously by Congress? Also, will Congress and the President allow FOGCO to operate without considering certain political realities; e.g., the necessity of making investments in several states, not just in those few where oil investments are likely to prove most promising? I have no doubt that a public corporation could be designed so that it would not be subject to these and similar pressures. However, in light of the fact that recent U.S. energy policymaking has been highly politicized, I have serious doubts that

FOGCO would be so designed. In sum, after assessing the likely answers to these three questions, I conclude that the establishment of FOGCO-type companies should be vigorously opposed.

Proposals for Specialized Public Oil Companies

In addition to proposals to establish a FOGCO-type company that would explore for and develop new petroleum supplies throughout the country, there have also been proposals to establish public companies that would be assigned more limited tasks. The two most prominent proposals in early 1975 were the suggestions of Senators Frank Church and Philip A. Hart (subsequently endorsed by a majority of the House Ways and Means Committee) that the United States establish a federal agency that would act as the sole purchasing agent for all oil imports and the suggestion of Senator Ernest F. Hollings that the federal government contract for oil exploration of the Outer Continental Shelf.

The avowed purpose of the Church-Hart proposal was to get lower prices of foreign oil by forcing oil-exporting countries to bid against each other for the privilege of selling in the American market. Petroleum economist John Lichtblau has summarized cogently the reasons why establishing a federal oil-importing monopoly was unlikely to achieve this goal:

> . . . OPEC's most likely reaction to an American import monopoly would be to confront it with a single export price. . . . Thus, the proposed Federal oil import agency could well have the effect of strengthening OPEC's cartel policy. . . . What is to prevent it from turning the tables and submitting a collective bid above the prevailing world market price? Our only options would then be to accept the bid or do without OPEC oil. They know we can't accept the second choice.
>
> But suppose some OPEC member . . . did want to increase its oil exports by underselling its cartel partners. It would have to do so secretly so as not to be branded a saboteur. . . . There would be plenty of opportunities for such deals right now. International oil companies and other importers would love to buy oil below the official tax-paid cost. They would have every incentive to keep such purchases a deep secret. . . . Furthermore, such discounts can be given to the private companies in many hidden ways such as longer payment terms, rebates

on freight rates, favorable exchange rates or payment for service fees for operations the companies perform in the exporting countries. . . .

A Federal agency, by contrast, would be structurally far less flexible to take advantage of such indirect price reductions. But more important, the OPEC member in question would run a much higher risk of having a confidential price reduction publicly disclosed if the purchaser is a United States government agency than if it is a private commercial company. . . .

Finally, the proposed scheme would be an administrative nightmare. It would be all but impossible for a single agency to act as the sole purchaser of nearly 4 million barrels of crude oil daily for well over 100 American refining companies with many different quality requirements and logistical problems.[42]

The development of new petroleum reserves in frontier regions (i.e., the Outer Continental Shelf [OCS] and Northern Alaska) is an extremely risky business. It is widely believed that the presence of significant uncertainties results in lower lease bonus bids and hence in reduced government revenues. Studies of the rate of return realized on OCS investments (cited above) fail to support this belief. Nevertheless, I do find somewhat persuasive the rebuttal offered by Senator Hollings:

> Vice President James Carter of the Gulf Oil Corporation probably stated my concern best. I asked Vice President Carter whether, if Gulf Oil owned 10 million acres of Outer Continental Shelf lands and was preparing to sell it to Exxon, wasn't it fundamental that Gulf Oil explore those properties to determine a value before selling them to Exxon. He stated that there was no doubt about it. If this business practice is considered sound to protect the interests of stockholders, then why isn't the same practice by government to protect the citizenry considered sound? [43]

In order to protect the citizenry, Senator Hollings proposed an "Offshore Energy Production Plan" that had two principal features. One provided for experimental government contracted exploratory drilling in certain designated OCS areas. The second was a major revision in the procedures for leasing OCS lands.

The Hollings experimental drilling plan would require the government to sponsor in selected OCS areas

. . . exploratory drilling in the same manner that government con-
ducted its space program. That is, the government should contract with
the private or independent drillers to do the work, and the information
gained therefrom should be public.[44]

Having explored the land, it would then be leased to interested oil
companies who would be responsible for all development and production.

Under Hollings's revised OCS leasing program

. . . companies would bid on shares of a joint venture for exploring
and developing entire submerged geological structures (called traps)
with high potential for oil and gas. Leasing entire traps would eliminate
the need to hold exploratory data confidential and also would enhance
the efficiency of both exploration and production. Cash bids would be
placed in escrow for use in meeting exploration costs, thus reducing
"front end" capital requirements and permitting smaller companies to
participate in bidding. The government would receive a fixed share of
the net profits of the joint venture and would take part in the development of exploration and production plans. Total return to industry and
government alike would depend on the amount of oil and gas found.[45]

Senator Hollings has offered a constructive set of proposals for
reforming offshore energy production in the United States—they
merit serious public debate. Unlike most other proposals to establish
a federal presence in the petroleum business, Hollings's are much
more limited and far less inflammatory. Moreover, they hold promise
of alleviating the specific problems that they are designed to attack.
In my opinion, U.S. energy policymaking would be improved greatly
if serious public consideration were only granted to proposals that
satisfy this relevancy criterion.

CHAPTER EIGHT
Problems of Electric Utilities

ON APRIL 23, 1974, Consolidated Edison, the giant electric utility serving the New York City metropolitan area, announced that it was suspending payment of its quarterly dividend. It also indicated that unless New York State provided immediate aid by paying $500 million for two partially finished generators, its future financial viability was in doubt. Prior to the April 23 announcement, Con Ed had paid uninterrupted quarterly dividends for 88 years. Because of this enviable record, Wall Street had long rated its common stock to be a "safe" investment for "widows and orphans." Hence, Con Ed's surprising decision to suspend its dividend triggered an immediate reappraisal by investors of the future profitability and viability of the entire U.S. electric utility industry.

Soaring fuel costs and reduced electricity sales—both direct results of the OAPEC embargo—were principal causes of the electric utilities' immediate financial problems. Given time and higher rates to offset higher fuel costs, these problems were surmountable. However, beginning in the late 1960s, the viability of this industry was also threatened by two other problems that increasingly endangered its ability to provide adequate capacity to meet growing electricity demands: unanticipated delays in expanding electricity generating capacity and permanently deteriorating finances.

The delays in expanding electricity generating capacity had two principal causes. First, growing public concern about both the waste products that fossil-fuel turbines discharge into the atmosphere and the possible dangers of nuclear accidents made it increasingly difficult to find acceptable sites for new generating capacity. Second, construction of new nuclear power plants was taking several years longer than expected to complete—in 1973 only 21,000 of the 36,000 megawatts of nuclear capacity originally scheduled for completion were operational.[1] Moreover, owners of the operational nuclear plants found that they could not be relied upon because of frequent and long safety and maintenance shutdowns.[2]

Electric utilities enjoy impressive scale economies in production and, especially, in transmission. Unit production costs decline substantially for plant sizes up to 1,000 megawatts—a capacity sufficient to serve a city of several hundred thousand. Doubling a region's transmission capacity typically requires an investment increase of less than 50 percent.[3] The classic economic rationale for public regulation of electric utilities has been premised on the inference that the presence of such extensive scale economies entails that this industry is a natural monopoly: [4]

> That is, the minimum optimal scale of production is so large that there is room in a given market for only one or at most a very few firms realizing all production and distribution economies of scale. In other words, the long-run unit cost function declines continuously out to a scale of output which saturates potential market demand. A monopolist therefore can enjoy lower unit costs than a group of small-scale competitors would. To secure the advantages of size while preventing the firm from raising prices to levels which exploit its monopoly position, regulation is imposed.[5]

Electric utilities enjoyed falling unit production costs throughout most of the 1950s and 1960s because savings due to scale economies and technological improvements more than offset generally moderate increases in input costs. Hence, utilities discovered that they could earn higher profits without raising prices. "As long as prices were not going up, regulatory commissions were happy to 'live and let live,' engaging in little or no formal rate of return regulation."[6]

The statutes establishing most regulatory commissions mandate that they insure that electricity rates be reasonable and nondiscriminatory and that high-quality service be maintained. Subject only to common law and statutory law guarantees that their methods respect certain norms of fairness—in particular, that rates should be high enough to allow the regulated firm to earn a "fair" return for its owners—regulatory commissions have wide latitude in the choice of specific instruments and procedures for implementing this legislative directive.[7] Professor Paul Joskow has described the typical regulatory process during the 1950s and most of the 1960s as follows:

> Contrary to the popular view, it does not appear that regulatory agencies have been concerned with rates of return per se. The primary concern of regulatory commissions has been to keep nominal prices from increasing. Firms which can increase their earned rates of return without raising prices or by lowering prices . . . have been permitted to earn virtually any rate of return that they can. Formal regulatory action in the form of rate of return review is primarily triggered by firms attempting to raise the level of their rates or to make major changes in the structure of their rates. The rate of return review is then used to establish a new set of ceiling prices which the firm must live with until another regulatory hearing is triggered. General price reductions do not trigger regulatory review, but are routinely approved without formal rate of return review.
>
> . . . State commissions especially are oriented to "do nothing" if none of the actors in the regulatory process are complaining. Consumer groups and their representatives (including politicians) tend to be content if the nominal prices they are charged for services are constant or falling. Consumers see prices, not the rates of return earned by the producers. Especially in an economy where the average price level rises over time, consumers will be content with prices for a particular service that are constant or falling. Most regulatory commissions are aware of this and behave accordingly, leaving well enough alone as long as prices behave in this way. Regulatory reviews are therefore initiated by requests for nominal price increases and not by the drift of rates of return above some imaginary "allowed" level.[8]

Because of accelerating inflation and soaring interest rates, electric utilities' unit capital costs began to climb sharply in the late 1960s. Utilities had to absorb these capital cost hikes until they could persuade state regulatory commissions to approve higher electricity rates. To get permission they first had to complete a time-consuming formal regulatory review. Because of the speed of the inflation, rate relief based on cost increases incurred immediately prior to the formal hearings proved inadequate—new higher rates were necessary even before the review was completed. This tendency toward inadequate rate relief was exacerbated by the fact that state regulatory commissions faced increasingly effective consumer pressure not to allow a total pass-through of utilities' higher operating and capital costs.

Soaring costs prompted electric utilities to petition repeatedly for compensating rate hikes. Most regulatory commissions lacked sufficient staffing to deal with this sudden increase in workload. Making an already horrendous task even more difficult, both consumerists and environmentalists began demanding that the traditional purview of regulation be expanded to embrace a variety of other public problems. Thus, many consumer groups have argued that present rate structures should be inverted so that larger users pay higher (rather than lower) unit rates; some go further and urge that because electricity has become a necessity all citizens are entitled to receive some minimum quantity, even if they can't afford to pay for it. Similarly, environmental groups have endorsed changing rate structures so that electricity consumers bear the social cost of the output they consume. Moreover, they have also used regulatory hearings as a forum to advance the argument that regulators should be required to establish and enforce detailed siting criteria for new power plants.

The future prospects of the U.S. electric utility industry have deteriorated significantly since the late 1960s. Unless the growth in annual electricity consumption falls permanently below the 7 percent post-World War II average and inflation recedes far below 1974 levels, construction delays and inadequate finances will continue to plague this industry in the years ahead. Whether the U.S. government will adopt the monetary and fiscal policies necessary to cause a permanent slowdown in inflation is a question beyond the scope of this book. However, because post-embargo sharp rises in electricity rates do appear to be causing a substantial slowdown in the growth of consumption, the prospects of adequate future electric supplies are presently improving. Whether this very recent favorable trend continues or proves temporary will depend on the solutions offered by our policymakers to a variety of important questions presently facing this industry.

FUTURE PUBLIC POLICY ISSUES

New Generating Capacity: How Much? What Type? When? Where?

Electricity is a flexible and convenient type of energy: all fuels can be used to generate electricity and, in the absence of offsetting price differences, consumers prefer it in most non-transportation applications. Also, because of scale economies and technological progress, until the late 1960s the cost to consumers of electricity rose far more slowly than the cost of all other types of energy. As a result, electricity consumption grew at a 7 percent average annual rate from the mid-1930s to the mid-1970s—nearly twice as fast as the average annual growth in total energy consumption. Hence, over this 40-year period, the U.S. electric utility industry had to double its generating and transmission capacity every ten years.

The capacity of electric utilities totaled roughly 450,000 megawatts in 1974. Because of recent and anticipated near-future sharply higher prices, the future average annual rate of growth in electricity consumption should be far below past levels. Nevertheless, even if the future growth rate falls to half of its post-1930s annual average (i.e., to 3.5 percent), roughly 650,000 megawatts of capacity will be necessary to satisfy 1985 demands. One widely cited estimate of the cost of the 200,000 megawatts of necessary new electricity capacity is $242 billion in 1975 dollars.[9]

Coal, fuel oils, natural gas, and enriched uranium are the principal fuels presently used to generate electricity. Because domestic supplies of coal and uranium are relatively abundant, the Federal Energy Administration has urged that policies be adopted to facilitate use of these two fuels in new plants. The FEA's position is buttressed by the fact that, given current and expected future fuel prices, electricity is produced most cheaply in plants using these two fuels.

Because of the tight finances and slower growth of demand, in 1974 electric utilities either canceled or significantly delayed 170,000 megawatts of previously planned new capacity. Nuclear plants accounted for two-thirds of this cancelled capacity and most of the rest was coal-fired.[10] In the past, when utilities have canceled large nuclear or coal-fired plants, they have usually substituted jet turbines fueled by either high-cost natural gas or light fuel oils. This substitution is undesirable; in addition to being more expensive, the decision to produce electricity with jet turbines ultimately necessitates higher oil imports and therefore increased U.S. vulnerability to future oil embargoes.

Three factors were responsible for the electric utilities' apparently perverse decision to replace lower total unit cost nuclear and coal electricity generating capacity with jet turbines. First, jet turbines take about two years to install and currently entail an investment of less than $200 per kilowatt hour of capacity. In sharp contrast, installation of new coal and nuclear base-load capacity takes roughly eight and ten years, respectively, and the investment requirements presently exceed $500 per kilowatt hour of capacity.[11] Far lower fuel and amortization costs for coal and nuclear generating plants more than offset the lower capital costs of jet turbines. Nevertheless, because recently there has been enormous uncertainty about such important economic parameters as future growth rates of electricity demand, future levels of inflation and interest rates, and future electricity rates, it is not surprising that electric utilities wish both to delay making investment decisions and to choose the option requiring the smallest capital investment. The decision to cancel plans to build new coal or nuclear plants and (if necessary to satisfy growing demands) substitute jet turbines accomplishes both results.

Second, new construction of both coal and nuclear generating plants has provoked strong opposition from environmentalists. They oppose new coal plants because the problem of cleaning up air emissions has yet to be adequately solved. They oppose new nuclear plants because of legitimate concerns that such problems as preventing nuclear accidents and the theft of radioactive materials have not been and perhaps cannot be circumvented. Many electric utilities have discovered that the easiest way to avoid the environmentalists' attack is to cancel plans to build new coal and nuclear plants and, if blackouts become imminent, substitute jet turbines.

Third, electric utilities have encountered growing difficulty in persuading state regulatory commissions to approve rate hikes that fully offset higher capital costs. However, all states presently allow them to immediately pass on higher fuel costs to consumers.[12] Thus, present regulatory practices encourage utilities to cancel plans to install capital intensive coal and nuclear capacity and instead install jet turbines that have far higher but fully reimbursable operating costs.

Canceling plans to build new coal and nuclear base-load capacity has enabled the electric utilities to avoid or delay a variety of present problems. However, unless measures are taken to hold future electricity demand growth to rates less than any authorities presently predict, it will entail severe future supply problems. Because of construction time lags, utilities will ultimately be forced to install huge amounts of jet turbine peak-load capacity. By adopting this strategy, electric utilities may avoid future blackouts. However, higher generating costs and greater oil imports will be inevitable costly corollaries.

Subsidies

Soaring electricity rates and deteriorating electric utility finances have resulted in numerous proposals to subsidize electricity consumers and/or producers. To illustrate:

1. The chairman of the Michigan Public Service Commission has suggested that in order to reduce electric utilities' interest charges and thereby forestall future electricity rate hikes, the Federal Power Commission should be authorized "to establish an insurance fund and guarantee debt service payments on qualifying debt securities of investor-owned electric utilities." [13]

2. The chairman of the Consumers Power Company has urged legislation allowing "the federal government to purchase utility securities, thus providing financially troubled utilities with construction funds." [14]

3. There have been numerous proposals to have state or local governments produce electricity.[15] The rationalization for these proposals is not that the government corporations would be more efficient but rather that they will pay lower interest rates due to the fact that interest paid by state and local governments is exempt from all federal income taxes. Thus, advocates of this proposal are implicitly suggesting that federal taxpayers should subsidize electricity consumption.

4. Many have advocated that electricity be sold to poor consumers at less than cost.[16] Utilities have suggested that this subsidy be fi-

nanced by an energy voucher system analagous to the Federal Food Stamp Program.[17] Many consumer groups prefer "life line" rate structures designed to charge a heavily subsidized low, fixed price for all electricity used up to a certain amount: higher rates would be charged for energy use above that level.

As the above examples illustrate, many find electricity subsidy proposals attractive. Moreover, it is always especially difficult to oppose subsidies that are allegedly designed to help the poor. Nevertheless, there is one compelling argument for concluding that *all* electricity subsidies should be opposed: "At a time when national policy is encouraging the conservation of energy, it would be foolish to use the power of government to keep the price below the true cost of producing electricity." [18] The continuation of past rates of rapid electricity demand growth will inevitably cause the United States to suffer greater vulnerability to future oil embargoes (because oil imports will be higher), severe future electricity shortages, and severe future electricity-related environmental problems. The best way of avoiding these problems is to discourage growing electricity demands by charging consumers the full cost of this product. The fact that I advocate this no-electricity-subsidy policy does not mean that I oppose other government-sponsored steps to aid the poor. I do oppose special electricity subsidies because they are likely to be inefficient and they will certainly encourage higher electricity consumption.

Rate Reforms

Differences in the prices different classes of consumers pay for electricity have traditionally been based on alleged differences in the cost to electric utilities of providing that service. Generally, larger users have been granted quantity discounts on the grounds that (1) a large portion of electricity transmission and metering costs are independent of the total amount consumed, and (2) the presence of scale economies in both generation and transmission implies that total costs rise at a slower rate than a user's total consumption.

Since the late 1960s there has been ever-mounting pressure for two types of rate reforms: (1) reducing or eliminating quantity discounts (and possibly even inverting electricity rates so that larger users pay higher unit costs), and (2) establishing peak-load pricing. Chapter 1 has discussed the rationale for peak-load pricing. Here we need only add that several experiments to test its practical feasibility are now underway and at least one state public service commission (Wisconsin's) now embraces the spirit of this idea.[19] If, as I suspect, these experiments prove successful, peak-load pricing will be used with increasing frequency in the 1980s.

There are two reasons for the growing opposition to quantity discounts. First, both consumerists and environmentalists have argued that quantity discounts no longer reflect real marginal (i.e., incremental) cost differences.[20] Specifically, consumer groups have observed that, largely as a result of accelerating inflation, adding new capacity has raised rather than lowered unit electricity costs since the late 1960s. Since efficient pricing requires that users be charged the cost of incremental capacity (and assuming that prior to the late 1960s rate differences did reflect cost differences), it follows that quantity discounts should be reduced. However, because a large portion of the total costs of servicing any given customer (i.e., transmission and metering costs) are only loosely related to his total electricity consumption, this argument fails to support the inference that all quantity discounts should be eliminated if efficient electricity pricing is to be achieved. Other things being equal, the costs to an electric utility do not double when one customer uses twice as much electricity as another.

The environmentalist attack on quantity discounts has been based on the premise that, in order to prevent environmentally costly overconsumption of electricity, rates should be set high enough to fully cover the economic and social costs of producing and transmitting power. They then infer that quantity discounts ought to be opposed because they encourage environmentally wasteful consumption by large users.

The environmentalists' premise is valid. Indeed, their definition of social costs should be expanded to embrace not only environmental degradation but also threats to the United States' vital security interests. It follows that the federal government has a legitimate reason for imposing a surtax on all electricity sales in order to discourage its consumption and thereby indirectly reduce both environmental damage and U.S. vulnerability to future oil embargoes.[21] However, this premise is not sufficient to support the environmentalists' inference that quantity discounts based on real cost differences should be abolished.

A second source of opposition to quantity discounts has recently come from the electric utilities. Because electricity consumption per consumer has been growing over time, any given declining rate structure results in average revenue declining over time. Simultaneously, unit costs have recently been rising. The concurrence of these two factors has forced utilities to repeatedly request rate hikes. By eliminating quantity discounts or, even better from the utilities' point of view, by inverting present rate structures, the need to request repeated rate hikes can be reduced and perhaps eliminated.

In sum, because the total cost of electricity service does not rise as fast as consumption, the economic arguments for *eliminating* quantity discounts are specious. However, because consumer groups, environmental groups, and electric utilities all embrace the move to reduce, eliminate, or even reverse quantity discounts, continuation of this trend appears inevitable. This may entail some inefficiencies in the U.S. economy.

Possibilities for Competition

Economists generally agree that regulation of privately owned natural monopolies is essential to protect consumers from being charged a monopoly price. Regulation of electric utilities has been premised, in large part, on the factual assumption that the technology of this industry entails that they be natural monopolies. This assumption has been evaluated critically only in recent years. As a result of this evaluation, some are beginning to suggest that important parts of this business could be restructured in ways that facilitate competition.

Electric utilities have traditionally been vertically integrated; the same firm has generated electricity, transmitted large quantities from the power plant to bulk markets, and distributed power to individual customers. Professor Leonard Weiss recently examined the possibilities for competition in each of these sectors. He concluded:

> Most important regions could support enough generating plants to permit extensive competition if the plants were under separate ownership

and had equal access to transmission and distribution. The physical limits on the size of the market are set by transmission costs, which vary approximately in proportion to distance and inversely with the square of transmission voltages. As the power load has grown, extra-high voltage transmission . . . has become profitable, thus greatly reducing the impediment to long-distance transmission. . . . In the more populous parts of the country, the possibility of high-voltage networks makes it technologically feasible for plants anywhere in a wide region to supply any consuming center connected with the network, though cost will still vary with the supplier's location. Much of the new capacity intended to supply the largest load centers is, in fact, being constructed at points more than 100 miles away in order to use local fuel supplies and to reduce air pollution in the more congested areas. . . .

There seem to be sharply increasing returns to scale in transmission, at least within the range of voltage now in use. It follows that additional transmission lines beyond the number needed for reliability would normally be undesirable. Additional transmission is, of course, required as demand grows; but, due to the increasing difficulty of acquiring additional right-of-way, it is often created by the replacement of existing lines with others of higher voltage rather than by the construction of parallel lines. As a result, it is unlikely that much competition in transmission can be expected through the construction of additional facilities. . . . In short, transmission qualifies as a classic "natural monopoly." . . .

It is widely believed that interutility competition would involve excessive costs due to duplicate distribution plants. If so, this would rule out direct competition for most residential, commercial, and small industrial loads at the local level. Economies in distribution seem to arise from increased load densities and are little affected by the absolute size of distribution systems. . . . There would thus seem to be no technical barrier to the existence of many geographically small distribution systems in an area. Some direct competition at the retail level may be possible (if not prevented by state territorial assignments or antipirating laws) for larger industrial loads that are close enough to service area boundaries to make the extension of transmission lines across such boundaries feasible or where open land between distribution utilities is being developed. However, the main sources of retail competition will remain intermodal competition, competition to attract new industrial load, and possible "yardstick competition" in dealings with regulatory agencies. Both of the latter would be enhanced by the presence of many distribution utilities within a region, each with access to the various generation sources of the region on a competitive basis.[22]

If, as seems likely, additional studies support in substance Weiss's conclusions, then policies designed to reduce the electric utilities' vertical integration and to reduce public regulation of bulk power sales will merit serious public consideration in the late 1970s.

CHAPTER NINE

U.S. Energy Policy in the late 1970s

ENERGY POLICYMAKING creaked laboriously along during the first year of the Ford Administration (August 1974 through August 1975). Congress and the President were unable to agree on either the general nature or magnitude of the needed reforms and new policies. Nevertheless, the United States finally took some initiatives that began to lay the groundwork necessary for a viable energy policy. This chapter evaluates these initiatives and concludes that four lessons must be learned if the United States is to deal effectively with its energy problems.

MAJOR ENERGY POLICY INITIATIVES: 1974–75

Pricing of Crude Oil and Natural Gas

U.S. dependence on oil imports can be reduced only if its production of domestic crude oil and natural gas rises and/or its consumption of these two fuels is reduced. Realizing this, President Ford took his most important energy policy measure when he sought to abolish "old oil" price controls and urged Congress to pass legislation abolishing price regulation of new natural gas. (To prevent higher prices leading to soaring oil-company profits, the President also requested that Congress enact a windfall profits tax on oil earnings and excise taxes of $2 per barrel on crude oil and 37 cents per Mcf on natural gas.) Though plagued by disunity, the consensus among congressional Democrats favored keeping and, in fact, extending petroleum price controls. For example, in February 1975, key Democrats were talking about passing a statutory ceiling price of 75 cents per Mcf for natural gas (i.e., a natural-gas price equivalent to a crude-oil price of $4.20 per barrel), and Senators Proxmire and Stevenson introduced a bill to freeze old oil prices at $5.25 per barrel and roll back new oil prices to $7. Throughout the first half of 1975 there were repeated, but half-hearted, attempts at compromise. But the differences between Congress and the President were too sharp; impasse resulted. Nevertheless, as the months passed two trends appeared that suggest that the United States' costly experiences with crude oil and natural gas price controls may finally be approaching an end. First, because Congress could not override a presidental veto of its extension of the Emergency Petroleum Allocation Act, authority to set "old oil" price controls expired on November 15, 1975. Shortly before this deadline, Congress and the President agreed on legislation requiring an immediate rollback to $11 in the price of new crude oil but allowing the phase-out of all oil price controls over the next 40 months. Second, as reports circulated of hundreds of thousands of jobs threatened by expected sharp increases in the magnitude of natural gas curtailments during winter 1975–76, public sentiment against higher natural gas prices finally began to erode. By mid-1975 Senate supporters of decontrol of new natural gas were rumored to have 45 votes. And, the leading supporter of tighter controls, Senator Adlai Stevenson, no longer talked about a natural gas price ceiling of 75 cents per Mcf; a ceiling of $1.30 to $1.50 now struck him as more appropriate.[1] In November the Senate actually passed a bill allowing limited deregulation of natural gas. The House, however, remained strongly opposed. Hence the battle to greatly relax or, even better, end natural gas price controls is likely to be long and bitter. But, because of strong presidential backing and, as the shortage worsens, growing support in the Congress, deregulation of natural gas is no longer an academic pipe-dream.

Tax Policy

The virtual abolition of the percentage oil-depletion allowance was the one substantive energy tax reform during the first year of the Ford Administration. The Democrat-controlled Congress successfully demanded this reform as the price for passing the President's antirecession tax cuts. Percentage oil depletion had been attacked for many years because it was a highly inefficient way of subsidizing energy production—most of this tax cut ultimately was received as higher rents by owners of oil lands that would have been explored and developed in any event.[2] Prior to 1975 the abolition of percentage depletion had been forestalled by intensive lobbying by both oil land owners and by oil companies that had agreed to pay higher lease bonuses because they could use percentage depletion to reduce their federal taxes. Congress deserves praise for quickly eliminating percentage depletion when, because of the coincidence of sharply higher post-embargo profits on domestic oil production and reduced oil-industry political power, the opportunity arose.

Three types of petroleum tax changes were debated, but not passed, during the first half of 1975. First, President Ford and the House Ways and Means Committee proposed, respectively, new excise taxes on crude oil and natural gas and on gasoline. Higher excise taxes are an excellent tool for persuading petroleum users to make investments that will help them to achieve permanent reductions in consumption. However, largely because the proponents of new petroleum excise taxes failed to emphasize that the resultant tax revenues could be (and should be) rebated by offsetting cuts in other taxes, their proposals never received serious congressional attention.

To prevent "double taxation" of foreign income, U.S. tax laws grant a credit for foreign tax payments by American firms. To illustrate, if an American company earns $100 in a foreign country with a 40 percent tax rate, it pays $40 in foreign taxes. The United States grants that company a $40 credit toward its U.S. profit taxes. Hence, assuming a U.S. corporate tax rate of 48 percent, this firm's U.S. tax obligation would be $8.

Most of the payments for foreign oil are classified as foreign income taxes and thus oil companies are entitled to claim offsetting foreign tax credits. However, these "income taxes" are actually per barrel charges (i.e., royalties) unrelated to the oil companies' foreign production income. Adoption of proposals to force oil companies to classify these foreign taxes as royalties and therefore treat them as ordinary business cost deductions rather than tax credits would raise oil industry taxes roughly $1.5 billion annually. Proponents of this change argue that it would eliminate what is presently a $1.5 billion subsidy by U.S. taxpayers to the owners and producers of foreign oil. Opponents argue that because no other nation places "double taxes" on its oil industry's foreign earnings, elimination of the foreign tax credit would reduce drastically the ability of U.S.-based companies to compete in international oil markets. The issue is sufficiently complex to merit extensive additional study before promulgating any changes in the oil companies' foreign tax credits.

Proposals to tax oil-industry excess profits came from a variety of sources. Some wanted an excess profits tax to recoup the higher oil-industry profits earned in the immediate aftermath of the oil embargo. Others, including President Ford, wanted to prevent oil companies from reaping windfall profits once old oil prices were decontrolled. As of September 1, 1975, none of these proposals had come close to congressional passage. Because oil industry profits fell sharply during the first half of 1975 and because of the difficulty of designing and enforcing a fair and efficient excess profits tax, I feel that adoption of this type of tax legislation would have been both unnecessary and undesirable.

Oil Tariffs

President Ford realized correctly that it was necessary to adopt some substantive measures to enhance U.S. oil security by reducing oil-import dependence. Using authority allegedly delegated to him by the Trade Expansion Act, the President placed a $2-per-barrel tariff on all crude-oil imports. As chapter 5 explains, a much more efficient tariff would discriminate between oil imports from the different exporting nations by placing sharply higher fees on imports from those countries classified as insecure. However, though preferable on security grounds, imposition of a discriminatory tariff would require congressional approval. This was unobtainable because a congressional majority was unwilling to take any steps that would lead directly to higher oil prices.[3] Given Congress's fondness for talking about the need for sharp reductions in U.S. oil consumption but its unwillingness to adopt any measures that would yield this result by raising prices, the President was forced to use the only price-raising measure thought to be available without Congressional approval: higher oil-import tariffs.

In August 1975, a federal Court of Appeals ruled that the Trade

Expansion Act did not delegate to the President the power to pro-
mulgate higher oil-import tariffs unilaterally. Final resolution of this
matter awaits a Supreme Court verdict. Regardless of the resolution,
the President's oil tariff did have the desirable result of forcing a
reluctant Congress to realize that policies more substantial than self-
righteous rhetoric were necessary to alleviate our major energy problems.

Environment

Only two environmental policy questions received extensive attention during President Ford's first year: stronger federal strip-mining
regulations and weaker automobile emission standards. Congress
passed two bills regulating strip mining. Key provisions of both bills
required states to tighten their strip-mining standards in order to protect surrounding land and vulnerable watersheds and required coal
producers to restore depleted mines to their approximate original con-
tour and pay an excise tax on all coal mined in order to finance reclamation of abandoned mine lands. In addition, strip mining was prohibited in national forests and a mining and mineral resources
institute was to be established in each state. The President vetoed
both strip-mining bills because he thought the reclamation tax too
high, the research institutes an unnecessary bit of porkbarreling, the
total prohibition on strip mining in national forests too severe, and
the statute's language too ambiguous. Ford's reasons for vetoing
were legitimate. But, unfortunately, the absence of federal strip-mining legislation allows the continuation of some ecologically destructive mining practices and creates unnecessary confusion for coal producers who, as a result, have delayed making some of the large
investments necessary to develop new coal mines. Thus, the inability
of Congress and the President to reach a compromise on strip-mine
legislation represents a real policy failure.

The other major environmental initiative was President Ford's repeated efforts to persuade Congress to relax automobile emission
standards in order to allow manufacturers time to improve fuel economy and to minimize the costs due to the introduction of new pollution control devices. In June 1975 he recommended that Congress

allow present 1975–77 emission standards to remain in effect through 1981. Congress seems likely to allow some relaxation of the clean-air standards, but less than the President's request.

Strategic Petroleum Reserves

In 1975 Congress and the President cooperated in drafting legislation to allow systematic exploration of northern Alaska's giant Naval Petroleum Reserve Number 4 and production of up to 400,000 barrels per day of crude oil from Naval Petroleum Reserve Number 1 at Elk Hills, California. Elk Hills's crude-oil production is desirable because it will cause a corresponding, almost immediate, reduction in U.S. oil imports. Exploration of N.P.R. Number 4 is essential if the United States is to design comprehensive long-range plans for reducing its oil-import dependence. Unfortunately this legislation had not been passed by both houses of Congress as of November, 1975.

In mid-1975 the two branches of government were also cooperating on legislation to set up a national strategic petroleum reserve equal to at least three months supply of imported oil. Realizing that creation of this reserve would take several years, an interim program to require companies to store up to 3 percent of their imports or refinery throughput was also under discussion. The creation of large strategic petroleum reserves promises to be one of the most effective measures for neutralizing oil embargo threats.

Energy Independence Authority

On October 10, 1975, President Ford formally proposed to Congress that it establish an Energy Independence Authority (EIA). Over the next seven years, EIA would be authorized to provide up to $100 billion aid to private projects satisfying two criteria: 1) they contribute directly and significantly to energy independence and 2) they would not be undertaken absent federal assistance. EIA would not be allowed to give direct grants in aid. However, it could give credit advances and extensions, guarantee loans and other obligations, guarantee minimum selling prices, and purchase securities. Hopefully, most of EIA's expenditures would be repaid and the Authority is designed to cease operations in 1986.

Stated plainly, EIA is designed to subsidize a rapid expansion in production from high cost new energy sources such as oil shale and coal gasification and new construction of coal or nuclear-fired electricity generating plants. There are at least three reasons for opposing the creation of such an authority. First, the goals of EIA are not feasible in a ten-year time span. Unless aid is granted freely to all supplicants, it will take considerable time to decide what projects ought to be backed. Once authorized, completion of many of these projects will take longer than ten years. Second, since projects subsidized by EIA need not satisfy a profitability test, normal market incentives to develop the least cost energy supply options will be diminished and may be eliminated. As a result, there is likely to be a sharp but unnecessary rise in the costs of producing domestic energy. For example, the capital goods sector is likely to experience a sharp jump in demand because EIA subsidizes many capital-intensive new energy projects. Because it takes several years to expand the output of this industry, the ultimate result will be soaring prices for capital goods and, hence, windfall profits for their fortunate suppliers. Third, expanded production of oil shale, coal synthetics, etc. will cause substantial deterioration of the environment.

Miscellaneous Policy Measures

A great variety of other policy measures were suggested and debated during 1974–75. For example, both Congress and the President favored measures to promote fuel economy. Indeed, in mid-July 1975, the Senate voted to force automakers to achieve a 100 percent mileage improvement within ten years. Past experience with too strict mandatory motor vehicle emission standards suggests that legislation of this type is of dubious merit. Because of soaring gasoline prices, the automobile manufacturers already have strong economic incentives to increase gasoline mileage. The emphasis placed on fuel economy in their present advertising confirms their awareness of this incentive. Hence, if they are feasible commercially, automakers would adopt measures necessary to achieve a 100 percent or greater improvement in gasoline mileage even in the absence of any government policy to promote this goal. If they are not feasible commercially, eventually any government policy mandating such a mileage improvement would have to be changed. In sum, policymakers would be better advised to devote their attention to creating economic incentives that promote greater fuel economy by both manufacturers and motorists rather than by arbitrarily establishing potentially unrealistic mileage standards.

To conserve petroleum, the President requested legislation to require the use of coal or nuclear energy to fuel new electric power generators. Given current and expected future fuel prices, it is unlikely that oil would be used to fuel any new base-load generating capacity. Neither coal nor nuclear energy can be used to fuel the jet turbines that may be necessary to meet demands for additional peak capacity. Thus, legislation mandating the use of coal or nuclear power to fuel new electricity generating capacity is either unnecessary or unfeasible.

To encourage the nation's financially hard-pressed electric utilities to build more energy-saving coal and nuclear base-load generating capacity, President Ford endorsed a June 1975 labor-management proposal for a $500-million-plus package of electric utility tax cuts. The proposed tax cuts include raising the electric utilities' investment tax credit from 10 percent to 12 percent; allowing faster depreciation of utility assets, and letting stockholders defer tax payments on utility dividends if they reinvest these dividends in new issues of electric utility common stocks. There is no question that electric utilities do need financial relief if they are to complete necessary base-load expansion. However, policies designed to raise revenues by raising electricity rates would be preferable to a program of tax subsidies because they would encourage slower electricity consumption growth and thus less expansion would be necessary. Unfortunately, in the mid-1970s, federal policies to promote higher electric rates are not politically viable.

Finally, a great variety of energy-related business or regulatory reforms were suggested. Congressional liberals advocated establishing federal companies in one or more stages of the oil and gas business and the Senate came surprisingly close to passing a bill that would break up each of the 20 largest integrated majors into four separate divisions. Chapter 7 presents my reasons for opposing these "reforms." Congressional conservatives and the President have endorsed removing regulations (e.g., restrictions on truckloads and routes) that lead to unnecessary energy consumption. The elimination of regulations that lead to fuel waste is obviously desirable. However, past experience with efforts at regulatory reform suggests that to do this will entail a sustained political battle lasting several years.

LESSONS FOR THE FUTURE

The United States has been enmeshed in an energy crisis since the onset of the OAPEC embargo. Although triggered by this embargo, the fundamental cause of this crisis was the contradiction between economic, political, and technological realities and our policymakers' inappropriate responses. A less contradictory domestic energy policy has begun to evolve slowly since the advent of the Ford Presidency. (Sadly, chapter 5 concludes that the United States' international energy policymaking has not shown comparable improvement.) Nevertheless, four lessons must be continually stressed if the United States is to have an effective energy policy. The first is the necessity of determining precisely what ought to be the goals of U.S. energy policy and—in order to prevent our policymakers from being overwhelmed by too many considerations—ruthlessly excluding all extraneous issues. The second lesson is the necessity of developing policies that are responsive to changes in the fundamental facts upon which they are based. The third lesson is the desirability of reducing the uncertainty that currently plagues energy suppliers and consumers as a result of indecision by energy policymakers and their frequent and seemingly capricious policy changes. And, the fourth lesson is that the necessary restructuring of U.S. energy policymaking will take several years and that such a restructuring is possible only if there is strong Presidential leadership.

Government action is essential if the United States is to achieve four valuable energy-related goals:

1. *Guaranteeing access to secure energy supplies.* The principal threat to U.S. energy security is the demonstrated power of a group of large oil exporters to embargo oil sales. This danger will persist as long as two conditions are satisfied simultaneously: any coalition of large oil exporters has sufficient cohesion to maintain monopoly power and the United States remains a substantial oil importer.

Hence, policies for reducing the oil-security threat should be designed either to foster disintegration of the economic and political ties
that presently bind together the large oil exporters or to encourage
substantial increases in domestic energy production and substantial
reductions in U.S. oil demands.

2. *Reducing energy's high resource costs.* By reducing the productive resources that it consumes in obtaining energy, the United
States can have more resources available for producing other socially
desirable goods and services. Hence, policies ought to be designed to
facilitate increased production of the relatively cheaper (in resource
costs) domestic fossil fuels—Alaskan and OCS crude oil, natural gas,
and coal—rather than increased commercial production of much more
expensive fuels like oil shale, tar sands, and coal synthetics.

3. *Limiting environmental degradation.* Some degradation of the
environment or of public health and safety is a by-product of the
production, transmission, and consumption of all types of energy.
However, there are large differences in the amount of degradation attributable to different fuels. Increased production and consumption of
natural gas and crude oil presently places the fewest demands on the
environment and public health. Hence, greater domestic production
should be encouraged.

4. *Limiting undesirable changes in the distribution of income.*
Prices of all fuels soared in the aftermath of the OAPEC embargo. As
a corollary, there was a large transfer of income and wealth from
energy consumers to the owners (both domestic and foreign) of low-
cost energy supplies. The largest single portion of this income and
wealth transfer goes to the oil exporting countries. Except for adopting measures that may ultimately lead to either the dissolution of the
oil-exporting countries' monopoly or to reduced consumption of imported oil, the United States is powerless to reduce this part of the
energy-related income and wealth transfer. Because of higher cor-
porate profit taxes, lease bonus payments, and royalties, a sizable
portion of the higher prices paid for domestic energy already goes
into federal and state treasuries. Nevertheless, post-embargo higher
energy prices have led (or will lead) to income and wealth transfers
totaling several billion dollars annually to the owners of low-cost
energy reserves.[4] If Congress desires, the size of this income and

wealth transfer can be reduced by introducing higher taxes on energy producers or users and by rebating the proceeds to consumers via income tax cuts. However, considerable care should be taken to insure that these tax hikes are not so high as to discourage new domestic production.

All energy policy proposals ought to be judged according to how much they are likely to advance or hinder achieving each of the four goals just discussed. Unfortunately, many policies are likely to have mixed results. To illustrate, the adoption of policies to eliminate price controls on "old oil" and natural gas should advance the goals of enhancing U.S. oil security, reducing the resource cost (but not, necessarily, the price paid by consumers) of providing the U.S. energy supply, and reducing environmental damage. However, other things being equal, abolishing these price controls will lead to additional wealth and income transfers to petroleum owners and producers. And, policies designed to increase coal production are likely to have deleterious consequences for the environment. It is the duty of energy policymakers to weigh these offsetting benefits and costs. It is my view that obtaining secure and lower-cost energy supplies presently deserves more weight than the problems associated with environmental degradation and a "worsening" income distribution.

Judging how each important policy initiative affects the four goals will not be an easy task. Hence, it is important that the attention of energy policymakers not be diverted by extraneous issues. Two items not deserving of substantial high-level consideration are the repeated requests that strong steps be taken now to develop what are presently exotic substitutes for scarce fossil fuels (e.g., fusion and solar power) and the repeated unsubstantiated charges of monopolistic abuses by the large oil companies.

The second lesson is the value of energy policies that are flexible in the sense that they either adjust automatically or with modest administrative input to substantial changes in the underlying economic, political, and technological facts. This type of policy flexibility is important because, at any time, knowledge of these facts is ambiguous; moreover, with the passage of time these "facts" actually change as a result of both external events and accretions to public knowledge. Great inefficiencies will inevitably result if specific energy policies are not capable of adjusting to these underlying changes. Also, the coupling of factual uncertainty with ignorance about the actual consequences of policy changes means that it is presumptious to assume that policymakers have the talents to fine tune energy policy.

The desirability of having flexible policies whose success does not depend on a specific set of events occurring is readily demonstrable by the example of natural gas price controls. As chapter 1 explained, one of the reasons these were imposed was to prevent an income transfer from consumers to natural gas owners and producers. They did not cause harm as long as natural gas supplies were relatively abundant. However, as time passed the demand for low-priced, clean-burning natural gas grew but, because it was becoming less profitable, new exploration and development began to diminish. The ultimate result has been ever-worsening natural gas shortages. Of course, the cost of these shortages to the American economy, in terms of both reduced oil security and unnecessarily high energy resource costs, soared in the aftermath of the OAPEC embargo.

The third lesson is that unnecessary indecision or ambiguity by policymakers creates costly uncertainty for energy consumers and producers. A corollary is that frequent changes in established energy policies can create unnecessary uncertainty and may lead to costly obsolesence of some large capital investments. The long delay in receiving commercial quantities of oil from Prudhoe Bay and the unnecessary costs borne by automakers and electric utilities—because unfeasible timetables for meeting air-emission standards were relaxed only at the last minute—illustrate the costly consequences of energy policymakers' indecision and ambiguity. In 1975 the Federal Energy Administration promulgated regulations designed to force owners of 32 oil-burning electricity generating plants to spend $260 million to convert to coal.[5] Earlier owners of many of these plants had spent millions switching from coal to oil in order to satisfy federal clean-air standards. This switch from coal to oil and back to coal graphically illustrates how policy changes can create unnecessary obsolesence.

Unnecessary policy changes should be avoided. However, it is important to emphasize that this is not an argument for maintaining the status quo. Once available evidence suggests that an existing energy policy has failed, it should be eliminated quickly. Similarly, promising new policies or modifications should be introduced. But, because new policies frequently have unintended consequences, some preliminary testing is desirable whenever possible.

The fourth lesson is that strong presidental leadership is essential if the United States is to develop a set of flexible policies designed to achieve the four energy goals. Presidental leadership is necessary because regional differences have hopelessly fragmented Congress on most energy policy issues. Most important, citizens from oil states tend to endorse policies that promote higher domestic oil prices and lower federal oil taxes; citizens from oil consuming states (especially energy-short New England) argue vociferously for the converse. As was the case when civil rights legislation was being drafted in the early 1960s, few Congressmen can be expected to possess both sufficient confidence in their reelection chances and sufficient statesmanship to act in opposition to these regional political realities. Thus, it is fatuous to expect that any Congress—even one heavily dominated by one political party—will take the lead in developing and passing a tough energy program.

President Ford has displayed the inclination to implement a coordinated program of flexible energy policies. Moreover, he realizes, correctly, that higher prices for domestic crude oil and natural gas are the key to the success of any such program. Unfortunately, the President lacks the power to force such a program through a reluctant Congress. In addition, some Ford proposals—most notably the $100 billion Energy Independence Authority designed to subsidize development of high cost and frequently high-polluting oil substitutes such as oil shale and coal gasification—indicate that the President has also failed to fully grasp the four energy policy lessons. This suspicion is buttressed by the President's failure to recommend stronger measures aimed at attacking directly the source of the U.S. oil security problem, the oil exporting countries' monopoly power.

PROGNOSIS FOR THE NEAR FUTURE

Energy policymaking was at a crossroads in late-1975. On the plus side, an American President recognized, for the first time, the need for implementing tough measures aimed at advancing the four energy goals. On the minus side, a large congressional majority (including Democrats and Republicans) was unwilling to risk the heavy political costs from legislating any measures that would entail higher energy prices. Unfortunately, presidental use of the veto will not suffice to persuade Congress to implement a positive energy program. Because Congress and the President are nearly equally matched, inaction is the most likely prognosis for U.S. energy policy prior to the 1976 elections.

Notes

ONE PRELUDES TO THE U.S. ENERGY CRISIS

1. OAPEC is composed of the Arab members of the Organization of Petroleum Exporting Countries (OPEC). All of the major oil-exporting countries except Canada are OPEC members. Members of the OAPEC subgroup accounted for roughly 60 percent of OPEC's sales just prior to the start of the 1973–74 oil embargo. The OAPEC members never explicitly defined what would be a "pro-Arab" foreign policy. Their decision to embargo all sales to the Netherlands and the United States was apparently premised on the belief that these two countries were Israel's strongest supporters.

2. Exxon estimated that the worldwide crude-oil shortage due to the OAPEC embargo was 4.5 million barrels per day. Source: "Aramco Sees Rapid Restoration of Crude," *Oil and Gas Journal* (January 28, 1974), p. 94.

3. At the time of the embargo, most of the oil traded internationally was sold under long-term contract to producing affiliates of the major international oil companies. These companies paid large royalties and production taxes to the countries from which they obtained oil. In the weeks immediately following the onset of the OAPEC embargo these fees were doubled. Many of the oil-exporting countries held minority ownership of the companies that produced their crude oil. As owners they were entitled to receive a specified fraction of the oil these companies produced. This was called participation oil. During the embargo, participation oil was frequently sold on the spot market to the highest bidder.

4. See ch. 5 in Policy Studies Group, Massachusetts Institute of Technology Energy Lab, *The FEA Project Independence Report: An Analytical Assessment and Evaluation* (March 11, 1975).

5. Consumers and many politically powerful industries (e.g., automobiles, tourism, and electric utilities) suffered huge losses as a result of the 1973–74 energy crisis. On balance, it seems implausible that the Nixon Administration could have thought that the political gains because of sharply higher profits for "big oil" would offset the political costs owing to these losses.

6. These themes are discussed in greater detail in Mancke, *The Failure of U.S. Energy Policy.*

7. *Ibid.,* chs. 1–4.

8. In the United States, oil is owned by whoever "captures" it from the ground.

When the land overlying a specified oil pool has many owners, each faces an incentive to produce the oil as quickly as possible in order to prevent a neighbor from "capturing" it.

In sum, overdrilling is encouraged.

9. The basic allowable formulae were not geared to engineering or geological constraints. A few of the larger fields could have produced oil at a rate several times higher than the basic allowable.

10. Most important, the Connally Hot Oil Act prohibited the interstate sale of oil above the allowables set by state prorationing boards.

11. See M. A. Adelman, "The Efficiency of Resource Use in Crude Petroleum," *Southern Economic Journal,* 31 (1964): 101–22.

12. Prorationing still entails some costs since some fields can produce at rates higher than their basic allowable.

13. Mancke, *The Failure of U.S. Energy Policy* (ch. 4) describes in more detail what groups benefit or lose from different U.S. energy policies.

14. For elaboration see Paul MacAvoy and Robert Pyndyck, *Price Controls and the Natural Gas Shortage.*

15. 15 U.S.C., §717, Note 3 (1964).

16. *Ibid.*

17. Phillips Petroleum Co. v. Wisconsin, 347 U.S. 672 (1954).

18. Paul MacAvoy, *Price Formation in Natural Gas Fields,* p. 4.

19. The most recent and comprehensive analysis is Paul MacAvoy and Robert Pyndyck, *The Economics of the Natural Gas Shortage.* This study concludes that natural gas supplies demonstrate considerable price responsiveness.

20. Joel Dirlam, "Natural Gas: Cost, Conservation, and Pricing," *American Economic Review,* 48 (1958), 491.

21. Atlantic Refining Co. v. Public Service Commission (CATCO), 360 U.S. 378 (1959).

22. British Petroleum and Exxon are also partial owners of the Prudhoe Bay field.

23. United States Department of Interior, *Final Environmental Impact Statement: Proposed Trans-Alaska Pipeline.*

24. Trans-Alaska Pipeline Act of 1973, Public Law 93–153, enacted by Congress November 13, 1973, signed by President Nixon November 16, 1973.

25. El Paso Natural Gas Company subsequently proposed that Prudhoe Bay's natural gas should be shipped to Valdez, via a pipeline built parallel to TAPS, and then liquefied and shipped to the West Coast. Thus, it is no longer certain that a trans-Canadian pipeline will be built. Hence, some of the environmental arguments against TAPS discussed in the text are no longer valid.

26. See Charles Cicchetti, *Alaskan Oil: Alternative Routes and Markets.*

27. Donald De Salvia, "An Application of Peak Load Pricing," *Journal of Business* (October 1969), pp. 458–76.

28. The literature on peak-load pricing is extensive. Early articles include M. Boiteux, "Peak Load Pricing," reprinted in J. R. Nelson (ed.), *Marginal Cost Pricing*

in Practice, pp. 59–90; and Peter Steiner, "Peak Loads and Efficient Pricing," *Quarterly Journal of Economics,* 71 (November 1957), 586–610.

29. There have been several studies of power plant siting problems, including U.S. Office of Science and Technology, *Electric Power and the Environment* and Committee on Power Plant Siting of the National Academy of Engineering, *Engineering for Resolution of the Energy-Environment Dilemma.*

30. Appendix G in U.S. Cabinet Task Force on Oil Import Control, *The Oil Import Question.*

31. Prior to Occidental's request, Stewart Udall, President Johnson's Secretary of the Interior, had granted additional oil-import allocations to a select group of importers. Most important were grants of 24,800 barrels per day to Phillips Petroleum; 10,000 barrels per day to Commonwealth Oil, and 15,000 barrels per day to Hess Oil. Some charged that the decision to reward these companies with valuable additional allocations was politically motivated.

32. U.S. Cabinet Task Force on Oil Import Control, *The Oil Import Question,* p. 128.

33. Because U.S. crude oil demands were growing far faster than domestic supplies, sharp price rises would have been a corollary of any decision not to relax the import quotas.

34. Mancke, *The Failure of U.S. Energy Policy,* discusses several additional examples.

TWO   THE PERFORMANCE OF THE FEDERAL ENERGY OFFICE

1. The FEO was created by Presidential Executive Order 11748, issued December 4, 1973.

2. Federal Energy Administration Act of 1974 (PL 93–275, HR11793, enacted by Congress May 2, 1974, signed by President Nixon May 7, 1974).

3. October forecasts of the size of the embargo-caused U.S. crude-oil shortages ranged between 2.7 and 4.0 million barrels per day. By January the FEO was planning to deal with a shortage of 2.8 million barrels per day.

4. Year-round daylight saving time directly conserved no appreciable amount of energy. However, it did serve to dramatize the severity of the energy crisis and thus probably encouraged greater voluntary conservation.

5. See "FEO Seeks Relief on Crude Allocation," *Oil and Gas Journal,* (February 25, 1974), p. 28.

6. U.S. petroleum supplies had been tight throughout 1973. Prior to the Arab embargo too little refinery capacity was the cause of the supply stringency. For elaboration, see Richard B. Mancke, "Petroleum Conspiracy: A Costly Myth," *Public Policy* (Winter 1974), pp. 1–13.

7. The use of year-to-year comparisons automatically takes account of the seasonal variations in inventories of most important petroleum products. To illustrate, oil companies typically build up large inventories of the distillate fuel oils used in space heating during the summer and draw them down during the winter.

8. From the American Petroleum Institute's weekly refinery report, as reported in *Oil and Gas Journal* (October 15, 1973), pp. 180–81.

9. At the start of the embargo some OAPEC members (notably Libya) continued to ship some oil to the United States. Unfortunately, after this information was leaked to the press by government officials, the flow of "hot" OAPEC oil dried up immediately. Source: interviews with former FEO officials.

10. For reasons discussed in the text, the legislation authorizing petroleum allocation was actually written several months before the OAPEC embargo. Hence, a reading of the legislation does not suggest that the goal of allocation was to spread the burdens of the petroleum shortage in an efficient and "equitable" way. Nevertheless, after the embargo, this should have been and was FEO's goal.

11. No objective definition of an equitable distribution of the burdens of petroleum shortages is possible. Most individuals define as equitable all redistributions that benefit them. During the OAPEC embargo those interest groups with the most political clout tended to receive favored treatment. Thus, farmers and truckers were awarded higher allocations of petroleum products than less vocal consumers, and some refiners were subsidized by being granted the right to buy "cheap" crude oil from their competitors. See "FEO Revises Allocation Rules Again," *Oil and Gas Journal* (January 21, 1974), p. 38.

12. The FEO allowed gas stations that desired more gasoline than they were allocated by the general allocation rule because of special circumstances (for example, a sharp jump in their sales volume had occurred since the 1972 base period) to file "Form 17s." Thousands were filed. Unfortunately, inadequate staffing prevented the FEO from processing most of them. Hence, few exceptions were granted prior to March. The FEO decided to honor all Form 17 requests in March. As a result, by April the interregional allocation program for gasoline stations had been effectively gutted. Since the gasoline shortage was over, this was a desirable though unintended result. Source: interviews with former FEO officials.

13. This disincentive was eliminated in May 1973, when the President issued an executive order abolishing the U.S. Mandatory Oil Import Quota Program. By this time, several oil companies had already closed down retailing operations in large regions of the country.

14. Some dealers who had gone out of business after 1972 found that it was profitable to reopen during the OAPEC embargo. The allocation regulations required their former suppliers to resupply them. Source: interviews with former FEO officials.

15. To illustrate, because of higher raw material costs, most refiners were allowed to raise their prices by about 4 cents per gallon on March 1, 1974. Therefore, they held back on late February deliveries.

16. Source: interviews with former FEO officials.

17. This clause read: "Refineries required to sell crude oil under this program shall be allowed to increase their product prices to reflect increased crude oil cost of all available crude prior to making crude oil sales to comply with this program."

Reprinted in "Double-Dipping Oil Companies?" *Wall Street Journal* (September 17, 1974), p. 22.

18. U.S. crude-oil imports fell from a daily average of 2.06 million barrels in December 1973 and January 1974 to 1.71 million barrels in February and March. Part of this fall was due to a more effective embargo; part was due to the disincentives caused by the interrefinery reallocation regulations. Source: Weekly import statistics of the American Petroleum Institute, reprinted in the *Oil and Gas Journal*.

19. See "Allocation Bungle FEA Probe," *Oil and Gas Journal* (September 23, 1974), p. 112.

20. Source: interviews with former FEO officials and "FEA Bungling," *Wall Street Journal* (October 8, 1974), p. 28.

21. See "FEA Bans Costs Pass-through via 'Double Dip'," *Oil and Gas Journal* (October 7, 1974), p. 54.

22. One caveat is necessary. Some lawyers familiar with the Emergency Petroleum Allocation Act have told the author that they feel the FEO's interpretation of its congressional mandate was far too narrow.

23. Most stripper wells are owned and operated by small so-called independent producers. There are thousands of independent producers and they have a vocal and effective lobby. It was the independents (rather than the huge majors) who lobbied successfully for a congressionally mandated stripper exemption from oil price controls.

24. See "U.S. Crude Price Rollback Seems Certain," *Oil and Gas Journal* (February 18, 1974), p. 46.

25. See "NPRA Complains about Two-Tier Crude Pricing," *Oil and Gas Journal* (September 24, 1973), p. 82.

26. Gulf Oil brought an unsuccessful suit to abolish the FEO's interrefinery allocation rules based on the contention that they were confiscatory. New legal attacks were mounted against the Federal Energy Administration's enforcement of similar regulations in early 1975.

27. The FEO also could have avoided several problems in gasoline allocation if there had been no petroleum price controls. For example, gasoline prices would have been relatively higher in the Northeast, giving refiners an incentive to eliminate regional disparities in supplies. Similarly, the FEO would not have had to adopt interrefinery allocation rules.

28. Slowing inflation was the initial motivation of the Cost of Living Council for enforcing petroleum price controls. However, after the onslaught of the OAPEC embargo, the goal of preventing windfall profits assumed at least equal importance.

29. "U.S. Oil Sees Possible Profit Slowdown," *Oil and Gas Journal* (May 13, 1974), pp. 40–41.

30. A Federal Trade Commission report cited by the *Oil and Gas Journal* (February 18, 1974), p. 38, shows that, for the twelve months ending September 1973, oil refiners earned a return on equity of 10.5 percent compared with 12.4 percent for all U.S. manufacturing. Because the oil industries enjoyed special tax treatment (the oil

depletion allowance and quick expensing of many development costs) a comparison of unadjusted returns on equity may understate slightly the industry's profitability vis-à-vis other industries. However, it is unlikely that these adjustments would be sufficient to explain the entire difference in average returns on equity.

31. Jim West and Steven Kelley, "U.S. Oils' Profits Skid Sharply from Stellar '74," *Oil and Gas Journal* (May 5, 1975), pp. 143–48.

32. *Ibid.*

33. American steel, aluminum, copper, and petrochemical companies also enjoyed sharply higher profits in 1974. However, since their businesses were not embroiled in public controversy, few suggested that their 1974 profits were excessive.

34. Royalties and severance taxes typically take up about 20 percent of any rise in oil revenues. Inflation-caused higher production costs probably ate up another 5 to 10 percent of the $4 hike in the price of exempt crude.

35. Source: newspaper reports and interviews with former FEO officials.

36. Source: interviews with former FEO officials.

37. Other independent observers of the FEO appear to concur with this conclusion. For example, after attending the first meeting of the FEO's blue-ribbon Evaluation Panel on the Short-term Energy Situation, Walter Heller, chairman of the Council of Economic Advisers under President Kennedy, wrote in a letter (dated January 5, 1974): "With respect to personalities, both Simon and Sawhill make a very good impression. They were aware of the pitfalls in their data and in their public posture. As to the staff, their economists also made a good impression, but they are distinctly shorthanded for the huge job they have to do."

THREE   PROSPECTS FOR ENERGY INDEPENDENCE

1. *New York Times* (November 8, 1973), p. 1.

2. Federal Energy Administration, *Project Independence Report.*

3. Principal elements of an accelerated energy supply program are standardized and expedited licensing to increase nuclear capacity an additional 15 percent by 1985; opening Naval Petroleum Reserves 1 and 4 to full-scale commercial development; significant accelerated leasing of Outer Continental Shelf waters; accelerated oil-shale production, and expediting the flow of materials and equipment to the energy sector. See FEA, *Project Independence Report,* p. 46.

4. FEA, *Project Independence Report,* Appendix AIV, p. 204.

5. Those interested in a more detailed evaluation of the *Project Independence Report* should read Policy Studies Group of the Massachusetts Institute of Technology Energy Laboratory, *The FEA Project Independence Report: An Analytical Assessment and Evaluation.* The conclusions of this study group are similar in tone to the conclusions in this chapter.

6. See United States Senate, Committee on Interior and Insular Affairs, *U.S. Energy Resources, A Review of 1972,* pp. 205–67.

7. Sources: M. King Hubbert, *U.S. Energy Resources, A Review as of 1972* in U.S. Senate, Committee on Interior and Insular Affairs; *U.S. Energy Resources: A*

Review as of 1972, pp.1–201; J. W. Devanney, R. J. Stewart, R. Ciliano, *A Preliminary Estimate of the Domestic Supply Curve of Oil From Conventional Sources;* letter from B. L. Hilton, coordinator of strategic planning, Exxon U.S.A.

8. Devanney et al., *A Preliminary Estimate*, pp. 6–7.

9. The USGS issued sharply lower estimates of U.S. crude-oil reserves in mid-1975.

10. See "Total Wells Drilled in the U.S.—1974," *Oil and Gas Journal* (May 5, 1975), p. 302. Drilling levels would have risen even more in 1974 if there had not been shortages of steel well casing and drilling rigs.

11. For elaboration see Devanney, Stewart, and Ciliano, *A Preliminary Estimate of the Domestic Supply Curve of Oil*. The conclusion that higher prices will not lead to a large increase in inland 48 oil supplies should be recognized as tentative. Until recently, U.S. oil producers have seldom enjoyed prices that have risen more rapidly than the inflation rate. Hence, there is almost no historical evidence of the response of U.S. oil production to sustained higher prices.

12. Richard B. Mancke, *A Method for Estimating Future Crude Oil Production from the United States' Outer Continental Shelf*.

13. The United States had leased approximately 11 million acres of OCS lands through 1974. However, rights to nearly 5 million of these acres had expired.

14. Some idea of the relatively high productivity of the United States' OCS lands may be inferred from the following data. In 1969 total crude-oil production from leased federal OCS lands averaged nearly 61 barrels per acre. In contrast, total crude-oil production from leased federal onshore lands averaged only 3 barrels per acre. See R. B. Mancke, *A Method for Estimating Future Crude Oil Production*.

15. Source: letter from Gene Hurrin, Acting Chief, Branch of Marine Minerals Leasing, Bureau of Land Management, U.S. Department of the Interior (October 10, 1974).

16. J. W. Devanney, *The OCS Petroleum Pie*.

17. "Exxon Abandons Destin Well, No Further Drilling Planned," *Oil and Gas Journal* (June 16, 1974), p. 41.

18. See Paul MacAvoy and Robert Pyndyck, *Price Controls and the Natural Gas Shortage*.

19. See M.I.T. Energy Lab, *The FEA Project Independence Report: An Analytical Assessment and Evaluation*.

20. Federal Energy Administration, *Project Independence Report*, pp. 98–108. Power plant effluents would be passed through scrubbers where a chemical reaction would remove most of the sulphur.

21. Edwin McDowell, "The Big Battle Over Scrubbers," *Wall Street Journal* (February 7, 1974), p. 6.

22. Federal Energy Administration, *Project Independence Report*, p. 127.

23. Reported in David Brand, "Safety Systems at Nuclear Power Plants Might Not Prevent Accidents, Study Says," *Wall Street Journal* (April 29, 1975), p. 10.

24. Danforth Austin and James Carberry, "New Fuel Plans Falter Because of Inflation and Other Hazards," *Wall Street Journal* (November 14, 1974), p. 1.

25. The FEA's estimates of 1985 U.S. energy production may be inferred from Table 3.1.

26. Because coal, natural gas, and nuclear power are substitutes for oil products, the crude-oil price hikes triggered higher prices for these fuels.

27. This discussion paraphrases Richard B. Mancke, *The Failure of U.S. Energy Policy*, pp. 3–6.

28. Oil imports may rise substantially but temporarily between 1975 and 1978 because the United States is heading out of a severe recession and major new energy supply sources such as Prudhoe Bay won't be on stream.

FOUR   ENERGY AND ENVIRONMENT:
THE NEED FOR PRIORITIES

1. The level of real energy prices will be the most important factor determining whether U.S. energy consumption continues to grow after 1985.

2. For elaboration see Mancke, *The Failure of U.S. Energy Policy*, ch. 3.

3. Stephen F. Moore et al., *Potential Biological Effects of Hypothetical Oil Discharges in the Atlantic Coast and Gulf of Alaska*, p. 39.

4. Max Blumer et al., "A Small Oil Spill," *Environment* (March 1971), p. 7.

5. Moore et al., *Potential Biological Effects*, p. 43.

6. Blumer, "A Small Oil Spill," p. 7–9.

7. Don E. Kash et al., *Energy Under the Oceans: A Technology Assessment of Outer Continental Shelf Oil and Gas Operations*, p. 117.

8. *Ibid.*

9. In additional to major spills, the production of OCS oil continuously discharges small quantities of oil into the water. Though small in volume, this oil is of particular concern due to its continuous presence in the marine habitat. However, the precise effects of chronic oil pollution remain poorly understood. Its two chief causes: oil-water separators that aren't totally effective and small leaks in the pipelines that transport crude oil to shore.

10. American Petroleum Institute and Federal Water Pollution Control Administration, *Proceedings of the Joint Conference on Prevention and Control of Oil Spills* (1969), pp. 107–28.

11. Straw absorbs five times its weight in oil. Corn cobs and polyethylene foam are also used as absorbents.

12. American Petroleum Institute and Federal Water Pollution Control Administration, *Proceedings of the Joint Conference*, pp. 249–51.

13. Julian McCaul, "Black Tide," *Environment* (November 1968), p. 8. Laboratory experiments have demonstrated that many dispersants are more harmful to marine life than oil. Moreover, oil-dispersant mixtures are even more toxic.

14. Don E. Kash et al., *Energy Under the Oceans*, p. 76.

15. Because large oil spills result in lost oil and damaged equipment, the oil companies would have economic incentives to take measures to reduce them even if there were no environmental sanctions. Environmental sanctions strengthen these incentives.

16. Two studies have reached the conclusion that total spillage in U.S. coastal

waters would be essentially the same whether the oil is produced offshore or is imported. See J. W. Devanney and R. J. Stewart, *Analysis of Oil Spill Statistics,* Report to the Council of Environmental Quality, M.I.T. Sea Grant Report Number 74–20, pp. 118–19, 124; Don E. Kash, *et al., Energy Under the Oceans,* pp. 241–43.

17. OCS production in the Gulf of Alaska raises two special environmental concerns. First, weathering will be much slower than in other regions: The low temperatures imply slower evaporation and, in winter, with greatly reduced daylight, slower photochemical oxidation. Second, the near-shore location of many Gulf of Alaska sites raises the probability that any oil discharges will reach the ecologically fragile shore. Moreover, the Gulf of Alaska is a region with extremely adverse physical conditions: earthquakes, undersea landslides, tidal waves, and extraordinarily high seas and winds. The increased hazards of production and storage which this entails, coupled with the biological richness of the Gulf region, suggests that the question of Alaskan OCS development deserves particularly careful examination.

18. Elburt F. Osburn, "Coal and the Present Energy Situation," *Science,* CLXXXIII (February 1, 1974), p. 478.

19. National Academy of Science and National Academy of Engineering, *Rehabilitation of Potential Western Coal Lands.* This discussion benefitted from a term paper written by Robert Reynolds titled "U.S. Energy Policy in the Northern Great Plain."

20. Edwin McDowell, "The Big Battle Over Scrubbers," *Wall Street Journal,* (February 7, 1975), p. 6.

21. "FEA, EPA Split Widens Over Sulfate Emissions," *Oil and Gas Journal* (April 7, 1975). Estimates of the total capital cost of installing stack gas scrubbers run as high as $10 billion.

22. David Brand, "Safety Systems at Nuclear Power Plants Might Not Prevent Accidents, Study Says," *Wall Street Journal* (April 29, 1975), p. 6.

23. David Brand, "Nuclear Safety Debate Rages Over Reliability of Emergency System," *Wall Street Journal* (July 9, 1975), p. 1.

24. David Brand, "Safety Systems at Nuclear Power Plants," *Wall Street Journal* (April 29, 1975), p. 10.

25. *Ibid.*

26. *Ibid.*

27. David Burnham, "AEC Files Show Effort to Conceal Safety Perils," *New York Times* (November 10, 1974), p. 1.

28. For elaboration see Mason Willrich and T. B. Taylor, *Nuclear Theft: Risks and Safeguards.*

FIVE   INTERNATIONAL ENERGY PROBLEMS

1. To be successful an embargo must cause a net fall in world oil output. If an embargo is successful then even those importing countries that are not its targets would suffer reduced oil supplies because higher oil prices in the embargoed countries would divert to them supplies otherwise destined for non-embargoed countries.

2. For elaboration see Robert Aliber, *Oil and the Money Crunch.*

3. Morgan Guaranty Trust, *World Financial Markets* (January 21, 1975).

4. Edwin Dale, "The Invasion of Petrodollars," *New York Times* (March 22, 1975), Sec. 4, p. 3. Dale quotes Senator Harrison Williams.

5. M. A. Adelman, "Is the Oil Shortage Real?"

6. *Ibid.*, pp. 101–7.

7. Inferred from the testimony of Thomas Enders, Assistant Secretary of State for economic affairs. Mr. Enders reportedly predicted that "under the Kissinger approach . . . the U.S. may end up with energy prices somewhat above the $7.50–$8 per barrel blend of controlled and uncontrolled oil but lower than present prices set by OPEC." See "Price Shelter for High Cost Oil Mulled, *Oil and Gas Journal* (December 9, 1974), p. 31.

8. These examples are discussed in M. A. Adelman, *Statement to the Senate Foreign Relations Committee Subcommittee on Multinational Corporations.*

9. Bernard Gwertzman, "Milestone Pact is Signed by U.S. and Saudi Arabia," *New York Times* (June 9, 1974), p. 1.

10. William Smith, "Saudis to Increase Their Share in Aramco from 25% to 60%," *New York Times* (June 11, 1974), p. 1.

11. *New York Times* (October 13, 1974).

12. See "Saudis Hiking Not Cutting Buy-back Prices, Royalties," *Oil and Gas Journal* (October 21, 1974), pp. 76–77; "OPEC Crude-oil Prices to Rise Jan. 1," *Oil and Gas Journal* (December 23, 1974), pp. 15–16.

13. *Trade Act of 1974,* Title V, Sec. 502, paragraph (b) (2).

14. The two Latin American countries that were OPEC members—Venezuela and Ecuador—were especially provoked by this clause denying their exports trade preferences. They argued somewhat ingenuously that they had never embargoed oil sales to the United States and therefore should not suffer "discriminatory" treatment. They mobilized most of the other Latin American countries in support of their position by suggesting that in the future these countries might wish to participate in cartels that limit sales of other commodities. As a result, U.S.–Latin American relations did deteriorate. Assuming that other effective cartels are not formed, deterioration for this reason should be temporary. If they are formed, further deterioration would be inevitable in any event. In sum, the cost from some deterioration in current U.S.–Latin American relations is probably heavily outweighed by the benefit from dissuading other countries from joining OPEC-like cartels.

15. "Kissinger on Oil, Food, and Trade," *Business Week* (January 13, 1975), p. 69.

16. *Ibid.*

17. M. A. Adelman, *Statement to the Senate Foreign Relations Committee Subcommittee on Multinational Corporations.*

18. Source: *Message from the President of the United States Concerning Energy Resources* (Washington: April 18, 1973), p. 10. For evaluations of the United States' Mandatory Oil Import Program see U.S. Cabinet Task Force on Oil Import Controls, *The Oil Import Question;* and Richard B. Mancke, *The Failure of U.S. Energy Policy,* ch. 7.

19. A proposal for a differential tariff was first outlined in U.S. Cabinet Task Force on Oil Import Controls, *The Oil Import Question*, pp. 134–35.

20. A differential tariff would be more difficult to administer than a simple flat-rate tariff. To prevent cheating, the United States would have to create a task force that would monitor all major transactions involving oil shipped to the United States.

SIX   THE FUTURE OF OPEC

1. Adelman, *The World Petroleum Market*, p. 77.

2. Massachusetts Institute of Technology Energy Lab, "Energy Self-Sufficiency: An Economic Evaluation," *Technology Review* (1974), pp. 32–34.

3. *Ibid.*, p. 34. The resource cost of all U.S. oil will not be this high. For example, the resource cost of the average barrel of oil from Alaska's huge Prudhoe Bay field was estimated by the government (in 1969) to be only 36 cents at the wellhead. Also, the resource cost of much of the oil from the U.S. Gulf of Mexico will be less than $3 per barrel. Unfortunately, the United States does not have enough oil in these relatively low-cost sources to supply its demands.

4. The lag between a decision to raise Persian Gulf oil output and when that new output can come on stream will be as short as one year only if drilling rigs, pipes, storage tanks, etc., are readily available.

5. Adelman, *World Petroleum Market*, pp. 182–91.

6. Some argue that the higher world oil prices are caused by the fact that world oil supplies are being rapidly exhausted. This argument is false. Since 1946 annual additions to the world's proved reserves of crude oil have always been far higher than consumption. For elaboration see Nordhaus, William, "The Allocation of Energy Reserves," *Brookings Papers on Economic Activity* (1973), pp. 529–76; and Mancke, *The Failure of U.S. Energy Policy*, pp. 8–13.

7. These twelve countries accounted for 84 percent of the rise in non-Communist crude oil output between 1967 and 1970. This means that several countries not listed also made significant contributions to growing world oil supplies.

8. "U.K. May Be Oil-Sufficient by 1980's," *Oil and Gas Journal* (November 19, 1973), p. 30.

9. "North Sea Belt Adds to Its Growing List of Giants," *Oil and Gas Journal* (February 11, 1974), pp. 17–19.

10. "Initial Alyeska Capacity to Double," *Oil and Gas Journal* (July 22, 1974), p. 30.

11. *Ibid.*

12. Richard B. Mancke, *A Method for Estimating Future Crude Oil Production from the United States' Outer Continental Shelf*.

13. Harold Wilson, "Offshore California, Long Shut Down, Begins to Stir," *Oil and Gas Journal* (July 7, 1975), pp. 15–19.

14. For discussion of petroleum rents see Mancke, *The Failure of U.S. Energy Policy*, pp. 48–51.

15. *Ibid.*, ch. 6–8.

SEVEN   COMPETITION IN THE OIL INDUSTRY

1. Federal Energy Administration Regulations for Allocation of Petroleum and Refined Products, Section 211.67.

2. Public Law 94–12 (March 29, 1975).

3. The price was in excess of $10 per barrel. Total resource costs of most OPEC oil ranged between 10 cents and $1 per barrel. The oil companies paid all production costs.

4. William Nordhaus, "The Allocation of Energy Resources," *Brookings Papers on Economic Activity* (1973).

5. See M. A. Adelman, *The World Petroleum Market,* chapters 5–7; and Subcommittee on Multinational Corporations, United States Senate Committee on Foreign Relations, *Multinational Oil Corporations and U.S. Foreign Policy.*

6. Subcommittee on Multinational Corporations, *Multinational Oil Corporations and U.S. Foreign Policy,* p. 36.

7. *Ibid.,* p. 46.

8. M. A. Adelman, *Statement to the Senate Foreign Relations Committee, Subcommittee on Multinational Corporations* (January 29, 1975).

9. "Independents Claim Big Exploration Role," *Oil and Gas Journal* (April 21, 1975), p. 58.

10. James McKie, "Market Structure and Uncertainty in Oil and Gas Exploration," *Quarterly Journal of Economics,* 84 (1960): 569.

11. U.S. Federal Trade Commission, "Preliminary Federal Trade Commission Staff Report on Its Investigation of the Petroleum Industry." In U.S. Senate Permanent Subcommittee on Investigations of the Committee on Government Operations, *Investigation of the Petroleum Industry,* p. 23.

12. See Adelman, *The World Petroleum Market,* ch. 4; and Zenon Zannetos, *The Theory of Oil Tankship Rates.*

13. Adelman, *The World Petroleum Market,* pp. 105–6.

14. U.S. Federal Trade Commission, "Preliminary Staff Report," p. 23.

15. Pipelines may face significant competition from alternative modes of transportation, especially tankers and barges.

16. U.S. Federal Trade Commission, "Preliminary Staff Report," p. 26.

17. Leo Aalund, "Refining Capacity Registers Largest Nickel and Dime Jump in History," *Oil and Gas Journal* (April 1, 1974), p. 76.

18. Leonard Weiss, *Deposition for U.S. v. I.B.M.,* U.S. District Court, Southern District of New York (June 11, 1974), pp. 354–55.

19. Further evidence on the viability of small refiners can be inferred from the fact that in 1973 refiners with less than 75,000 barrels daily capacity accounted for 39.4 percent of total expansion. See Leo Aalund, "A Close Look at Added New Refining Capacity in U.S.," *Oil and Gas Journal* (April 18, 1974), p. 33.

20. U.S. Federal Trade Commission, "Preliminary Staff Report," p. 21.

21. See *Oil and Gas Journal* (February 18, 1974), p. 38. For more elaboration

see Edward Erickson and Robert Spann, "The U.S. Petroleum Industry," in Edward Erickson and Leonard Waverman, *The Energy Question,* 2: 6–12.

22. Edward Mitchell, *U.S. Energy Policy: A Primer,* p. 91.

23. Mitchell comments: "One criticism of this approach is that initial period stock prices may already capitalize future monopoly profits. Therefore, rates or return calculated on initial stock prices would only reflect normal rates of return, even though monopoly profits were being earned. . . . As a practical matter this probably has little effect on our calculated rates of return. Any monopoly profits earned in the petroleum industry would . . . require lax antitrust and regulatory policy and a passive Congress and executive. The uncertainty of future public policy would mean that these monopoly profits would be discounted at a very high rate and that monopoly profits that might accrue four or five years in the future would be accorded a very small value in present stock prices. . . . Monopoly profits earned continuously for a couple of decades should definitely show up in our figures." Mitchell, *U.S. Energy Policy,* pp. 92–93.

24. *Ibid.,* pp. 93, 95.

25. See Jesse Markham, "The Competitive Effects of Joint Bidding by Oil Companies for Offshore Lease Sales," in Jesse Markham and Gustav Papanek, eds., *Industrial Organization and Economic Development,* pp. 116–35; Edward Erickson and Robert Spann, "The U.S. Petroleum Industry," in E. Erickson and L. Waverman, *The Energy Question,* vol. 2; and C. J. Jirik, *Composition of the Offshore U.S. Petroleum Industry and Estimated Cost of Producing Petroleum in the Gulf of Mexico.*

26. L. K. Weaver, et al., *Composition of Offshore U.S. Petroleum Industry.*

27. E. Erickson and R. Spann, "The U.S. Petroleum Industry," p. 17.

28. This argument was developed initially by de Chazeau and Kahn. Recent adherents include the Federal Trade Commission. See Melvin de Chazeau and Alfred Kahn, *Integration and Competition in the Petroleum Industry,* pp. 221–29.

29. U.S. Federal Trade Commission, "Preliminary Staff Report," p. 43.

30. *Ibid.,* pp. 17, 43.

31. *Ibid.,* p. 15.

32. *Ibid.,* p. 17.

33. The proof can be found in Mancke, *The Failure of U.S. Energy Policy,* note 33 to ch. 7.

34. *Ibid.,* note 36 to ch. 7.

35. This discussion relies heavily on American Enterprise Institute, *Federal Oil and Gas Corporation Proposals.* See *Congressional Record,* October 1, 1973, p. S18142.

36. Title VI-No. 643, an amendment to S2506.

37. *Congressional Record,* November 7, 1973, p. S20034.

38. *Ibid.*

39. *Ibid.*

40. Statement of John E. Swearingen before the U.S. Senate Commerce Committee (February 5, 1974), p. 7.

41. Statement of Frank N. Ikard before the U.S. Senate Commerce Committee (December 18, 1973), p. 27.

42. John Lichtblau, "Uncle Sam Would Be a Weak Oil Bargainer," *New York Times* (April 20, 1975), Sec. 3, p. 4.

43. Senator Ernest Hollings, "Speech Before the Petroleum Equipment Suppliers Association" (April 14, 1975).

44. *Ibid.*

45. Senator Hollings, "News Release" (April 14, 1975).

EIGHT   PROBLEMS OF ELECTRIC UTILITIES

1. Federal Energy Office, *Project Independence Report,* p. 119.

2. To illustrate, in January 1975, because of the discovery of cracks in the emergency cooling system of an atomic reactor, the Nuclear Regulatory Commission ordered utilities operating half of the nation's reactors to shut them down within 20 days. See David Burnham, "Defect in a Reactor Leads U.S. to Order 23-Plant Shutdown," *New York Times* (January 30, 1975), p. 1; Burnham, "Federal Study Charges Little Concern by Utilities with Reactor Reliability" *New York Times* (March 9, 1975), p. 42.

3. Frederick M. Scherer, *Industrial Market Structure and Economic Performance,* p. 520.

4. This inference has not been unchallenged. See Harold Demsetz, "Why Regulate Utilities?" *Journal of Law and Economics,* 11 (1968): 55–65.

5. Scherer, *Industrial Market Structure,* pp. 519–20.

6. Paul Joskow, "Inflation and Environmental Concern: Structural Change in the Process of Public Utility Regulation," *Journal of Law and Economics,* 17 (October 1974): p. 312.

7. A list of important precedents would include *Smyth v. Ames et al.,* 169 U.S. 466 (1968) and *Federal Power Commission v. Hope Natural Gas Company,* 320 U.S. 591 (1944).

8. Joskow, "Inflation and Environmental Concern," pp. 298–99.

9. "Utilities: Weak Point in the Energy Future," *Business Week* (January 20, 1975), p. 46.

10. *Ibid.*

11. Coal and nuclear plants are designed to run most of the time—they are said to supply base-load capacity. Jet turbines can only be run for brief periods of peak demand.

12. Use of fuel adjustment charges prevented total chaos when electric utilities' residual fuel oil costs had an eightfold increase in the months immediately following the OAPEC embargo.

13. William Rosenberg, "Utilities Need Help—Now," *Wall Street Journal* (January 8, 1975), p. 12.

14. "Consumers Power Wants the U.S. to Buy Utility Securities," *Wall Street Journal* (January 14, 1975), p. 13.

15. For example see Public Power Corporation Study Commission for Mas-

sachusetts, *Feasibility and Benefits of a Public Power Corporation for Massachusetts,* (February 1975).

16. See Reginald Stuart, "Utilities Embrace Energy Stamps," *New York Times* (April 27, 1975), Sec. 3, p. 3.

17. For a discussion of the inefficiencies of the Federal Food Stamp Program see Kenneth Clarkson, *Food Stamps and Nutrition.*

18. Murray Weidenbaum, "The Future of Electric Utilities," *Challenge* (January–February 1975).

19. See Thomas Bray, "Rate Test Affects Vermonters' Habits," *Wall Street Journal* (April 1, 1975), p. 28; "FEA to Fund a Utility Rate Experiment that Charges More for Peak-Hour Usage," *Wall Street Journal* (March 25, 1975), p. 12; Reginald Stuart, "Utility-Regulation Reform," *New York Times* (December 8, 1974), Sec. 3, p. 3.

20. In practice, rate differences have always been highly arbitrary. Joskow has written of the rate-setters: "They were primarily engineers who had evolved some mysterious mechanism for establishing rates. The concept of marginal cost was extremely difficult for them to understand. They were now being called on to explain and justify the methodology that they used for establishing rates and any meaningful methodology often appeared lacking—new rates were often across-the-board percentage markups of the existing rate structures." Source: Joskow, "Inflation and Environmental Concern," p. 318.

21. An electricity surtax on individuals could be either proportional to consumption or progressive. A progressive tax could be defended on grounds similar to those offered in defense of a progressive income tax. The tax on industrial and institutional users should be at a flat rate—it would be inefficient to charge General Motors higher rates than Chrysler merely because it is bigger.

22. Leonard Weiss, "Antitrust in the Electric Power Industry," in Almarin Phillips, ed., *Promoting Competition in Regulated Markets,* pp. 136, 144–46.

NINE   U.S. ENERGY POLICY IN THE LATE 1970s

1. Gene Kinney, "Gas Regulation Advocates Put on Defensive," *Oil and Gas Journal* (July 28, 1975), p. 57.

2. For elaboration see Mancke, *The Failure of U.S. Energy Policy,* pp. 77–87.

3. Congress did debate plans to limit U.S. oil imports by reimposing import quotas and, to prevent this from leading to higher domestic oil prices, enforcing stricter price controls. Of course, since prices would not be allowed to rise to market clearing levels, adoption of this policy would also require imposition of some type of rationing.

4. In late December 1975, President Ford signed an omnibus energy bill that mandates price controls on domestic crude oil until June 1979. This has reduced greatly the size of the income transfer to owners of crude oil. If old oil-price controls are abolished and no offsetting taxes are imposed, huge profits will be reaped by the owners of old oil. Higher energy prices have also led to huge transfers of wealth to the owners of other fuels. For example, both newspaper articles and TV news specials have featured

the soaring wealth reaped since the embargo by owners of small Appalachian coal fields. Until the embargo, many of these coal owners were impoverished.

5. Sanford Jacobs, "Law Forcing Utilities to Convert to Coal Stirs Many Objections," *Wall Street Journal* (June 26, 1975), p. 1.

Bibliography

Adelman, Morris A. "Efficiency of Resource Use in Crude Petroleum," *Southern Economics Journal* (1964), vol. 31.
—— "Is the Oil Shortage Real?" *Foreign Policy* (1972), vol. 9.
—— *Statement to the Senate Foreign Relations Committee Subcommittee on Multinational Corporations*. Washington: January 29, 1975.
—— *The World Petroleum Market*. Baltimore: Johns Hopkins Press, 1972.
Aliber, Robert. *Oil and the Money Crunch*. Chicago: University of Chicago Graduate School of Business, 1974.
American Enterprise Institute Legislative Analysis. *Federal Oil and Gas Corporation Proposals*. Washington: American Enterprise Institute, 1974.
American Petroleum Institute and Federal Water Pollution Control Administration. *Proceedings of the Joint Conference on Prevention and Control of of Oil Spills*. Washington: American Petroleum Institute, 1969.
Blumer, Max et al. "A Small Oil Spill," *Environment,* 13 (1971).
Boiteux, M. "Peak Load Pricing." In J. R. Nelson, ed. *Marginal Cost Pricing in Practice*. Englewood Cliffs, N.J.: Prentice-Hall, 1964.
Cicchetti, Charles. *Alaskan Oil: Alternative Routes and Markets*. Baltimore: Johns Hopkins Press, 1972.
de Chazeau, Melvin and Alfred Kahn. *Integration and Competition in the Petroleum Industry*. New Haven: Yale University Press, 1959.
Demsetz, Harold. "Why Regulate Utilities?" *Journal of Law and Economics* (1968), vol. 11.
De Salvia, Donald. "An Application of Peak Load Pricing," *Journal of Business* (1969), vol. 42.
Devanney, J. W. *The OCS Petroleum Pie*. Cambridge, Mass.: M.I.T. Department of Ocean Engineering, 1974.
Devanney, J. W. and R. J. Stewart. *Analysis of Oil Spill Statistics*. Report to the Council of Environmental Quality, M.I.T. Sea Grant Report Number 74-20, 1974.
Devanney, J. W., R. J. Stewart, and R. Ciliano. *A Preliminary Estimate of*

the Domestic Supply Curve of Oil from Conventional Sources. Marting-
dale Report to Mathematica for the Environmental Protection Agency,
February 20, 1975.

Dirlam, Joel. "Natural Gas: Cost, Conservation, and Pricing." *American
Economic Review,* XLVIII (1958).

Erickson, Edward and Robert Spann. "The U.S. Petroleum Industry." In
Erickson, Edward, and Leonard Waverman, eds., *The Energy Question,*
vol. 2. Toronto: University of Toronto Press, 1974.

Hubbert, M. King. "U.S. Energy Resources, A Review as of 1972." In
U.S. Senate Committee on Interior and Insular Affairs. *U.S. Energy
Resources: A Review as of 1972.* Washington, 1974.

Hudson, E. A. and Dale Jorgenson. "U.S. Energy Policy and Economic
Growth, 1975–2000," *Bell Journal of Economics and Management
Science* (1974), vol. 5.

Jirik, C. J. *Composition of the Offshore U.S. Petroleum Industry and the
Estimated Cost of Producing Petroleum in the Gulf of Mexico.* In U.S.
Department of Interior, Information Circular 8557. Washington: Govern-
ment Printing Office, 1972.

Joskow, Paul. "Inflation and Environmental Concern; Structural Change in
the Process of Public Utility Regulation," *Journal of Law and Economics*
(1974), vol. 17.

Kash, Don E. et al. *Energy Under the Oceans: A Technology Assessment of
Outer Continental Shelf Oil and Gas Operations.* Norman: University of
Oklahoma Press, 1973.

Lichtblau, John. "Uncle Sam Would Be a Weak Oil Bargainer," *New York
Times* (April 20, 1975).

MacAvoy, Paul W. *Price Formation in Natural Gas Fields.* New Haven:
Yale University Press, 1962.

MacAvoy, Paul and Robert Pyndyck. *The Economics of the Natural Gas
Shortage.* Amsterdam: North Holland, forthcoming 1975.

—— *Price Controls and the Natural Gas Shortage.* Washington: American
Enterprise Institute, 1975.

MacAvoy, Paul W., Bruce E. Stangle, and Jonathan B. Tepper. "The Federal Energy Office as Regulator of the Energy Crisis," *Technology Review,* 77 (1975).

Mancke, Richard B. "Genesis of the U.S. Energy Crisis." In Joseph Szyiowicz and Bard O'Neill, eds., *The Energy Crisis and U.S. Foreign Policy.*
New York: Praeger, 1975.

—— *The Failure of U.S. Energy Policy.* New York: Columbia University
Press, 1974.

—— "The Future of OPEC," *Journal of Business,* 48 (1975).

—— *A Method for Estimating Future Crude Oil Production from the United States' Outer Continental Shelf.* Medford, Mass.: Fletcher School of Law and Diplomacy, Tufts University, 1975.

—— "Oil and the National Security." In U.S. Senate Committee on Interior and Insular Affairs, *Issues Attendant to Current and Projected Reliance on Oil and Gas Imports.* Washington: January 10, 11, and 22, 1973.

—— *Performance of the Federal Energy Office.* Washington: American Enterprise Institute, 1975.

—— "Petroleum Conspiracy: A Costly Myth," *Public Policy* (1974), vol. 22.

Markham, Jesse. "The Competitive Effects of Joint Bidding By Oil Companies for Offshore Lease Sales." In Markham, Jesse and Gustav Papanek, eds., *Industrial Organization and Economic Development.* Boston: Houghton Mifflin, 1970.

Massachusetts Institute of Technology Energy Lab. "Energy Self-Sufficiency: An Economic Evaluation," *Technology Review* (1974), vol. 76.

—— *The FEA Project Independence Report: An Analytical Assessment and Evaluation.* Cambridge, Mass.: M.I.T. Energy Lab, 1975.

McCaul, Julian. "Black Tide," *Environment* (1968), vol. 10.

McKie, James. "Market Structure and Uncertainty in Oil and Gas Exploration," *Quarterly Journal of Economics* (1960), vol. 84.

Mitchell, Edward. *U.S. Energy Policy: A Primer.* Washington: American Enterprise Institute, 1974.

Moore, Stephen F. *Potential Biological Effects of Hypothetical Oil Discharges in the Atlantic Coast and Gulf of Alaska.* Report to the Council on Environmental Quality. M.I.T. Sea Grant Report Number 74-19, 1974.

Morgan Guaranty Trust Company. *World Financial Markets.* New York: January 21, 1975.

National Academy of Engineering Committee on Power Plant Siting. *Engineering for Resolution of the Energy-Environment Dilemma.* Washington: National Academy of Engineering, 1972.

National Academy of Science and National Academy of Engineering. *Rehabilitation of Potential Western Coal Lands.* Cambridge, Mass.: Ballinger Publishing, 1973.

Nordhaus, William. "The Allocation of Energy Reserves," *Brookings Papers on Economic Activity* (1973), vol. 3.

Osborn, Elburt F. "Coal and the Present Energy Situation," *Science* (February 1974), vol. 183.

Scherer, Frederick M. *Industrial Market Structure and Economic Performance.* Chicago: Rand McNally, 1970.

Steiner, Peter. "Peak Loads and Efficient Pricing," *Quarterly Journal of Economics* (1957), vol. 71.

United States Cabinet Task Force on Oil Import Controls. *The Oil Import Question.* Washington: Government Printing Office, 1970.

United States Department of Interior. *An Analysis of the Economic and Security Aspects of the Trans-Alaska Pipeline.* Washington, 1972.

United States Federal Energy Administration. *Project Independence Report.* Washington: 1974.

United States Federal Trade Commission. "Preliminary Federal Trade Commission Staff Report on Its Investigation of the Petroleum Industry." In U.S. Senate Permanent Subcommittee on Investigations of the Committee on Government Operations, *Investigation of the Petroleum Industry.* Washington: Government Printing Office, 1973.

United States Office of Science and Technology. *Electric Power and the Environment.* Washington, 1970.

United States President. *Message from the President of the United States Concerning Energy Resources.* Washington: April 18, 1973.

United States Senate. Committee on Foreign Relations, Subcommittee on Multinational Corporations. *Multinational Oil Corporations and U.S. Foreign Policy.* Washington: U.S. Government Printing Office, 1975.

—— Committee on Interior and Insular Affairs. *U.S. Energy Resources: A Review as of 1972.* Washington, 1974.

Weidenbaum, Murray. "The Future of Electric Utilities," *Challenge,* (1975).

Weiss, Leonard. "Antitrust in the Electric Power Industry." In Phillips, Almarin, ed. *Promoting Competition in Regulated Markets.* Washington: Brookings Institution, 1975.

—— *Deposition for U.S. vs. I.B.M.* U.S. District Court, Southern District of New York (June 11, 1974).

Willrich, Mason and T. B. Taylor. *Nuclear Theft: Risks and Safeguards.* Cambridge, Mass.: Ballinger Publishing, 1974.

Zannetos, Zenon. *The Theory of Oil Tankship Rates.* Cambridge, Mass.: M.I.T. Press, 1966.

INDEX

180

Federal Oil and Gas Company (FOGCO), 127–32
Federal Power Commission (FPC), 8–10, 19, 57
Federal Trade Commission (FTC), 116, 118, 121, 123–25
Ford, President Gerald R., 88, 100, 145, 146–53, 157–58

Geological Survey, U.S., 50, 76

Hart, Senator Philip A., 130
Hollings, Senator Ernest F., 130–32
Hubbert, M. King, 50

Interior, U.S. Department of, 10–11, 19, 55, 57
International Energy Agency (IEA), 86
International relations, U.S., 3, 12, 47, 81–91; Tehran Conference, 18; Saudi-American agreement, 84
Interstate Commerce Commission (ICC), 115

Joskow, Paul, 135

Kennedy, Senator Edward, 17
Kissinger, Secretary of State Henry, 85, 87–88

Legislation, U.S.: Clean Air Act of 1970, 14; Trade Act of 1974, 87; Sherman Antitrust Act, 106–8; Emergency Petroleum Allocation Act, 146
Lewis, Harold, 78
Lichtblau, John, 130–31

MacAvoy, Paul, 9, 59
Marketing, 118–19
McKie, James, 111–12
Military intervention, 87–88
Mitchell, Edward, 120–21
Monopoly, OPEC, 85, 93, 95–97, 101–3,

110–11; oil company, 105–32, 155; evidence of, 105–6, 111–27; natural, 134
Muskie, Senator Edmund, 17

National Science Foundation (NSF), 61
National security, 3–4, 82–91, 153–54; Alaskan pipeline, 12; oil imports, 17–18; military intervention, 87–88
Natural gas, 7–10, 29, 57–59, 146; shortages, 7–10
Natural Gas Act of 1938, 8–9
Nixon, President Richard M., 16–18, 21, 47–48
North Sea, 53, 94, 98–99
Nuclear power, 14, 61–62, 77–79, 133–34; safety, 77–79; theft, 77, 79; proliferation, 77, 79; disposal, 77–79; terrorism, 77, 79

OAPEC, 3, 21–26, 28, 36, 38, 47–48, 63, 81–91, 93, 101, 105, 156
Oil companies, monopolistic, 4, 105–31; Occidental, 16–17; major, 32–35, 40, 112–14, 116–27; others, 32–35; profits, 40–41, 119–23, 145; vertically integrated, 105; internationals, 108–11
Oil depletion allowance, 105, 123–26, 146–47
Oil imports, 3, 4, 10, 14–18, 21–27, 66, 88–91; Mandatory Oil Import Program, 90
Oil spills, 68–73; West Falmouth, 69–70; Santa Barbara, 69–70; blowouts, 71; *Torrey Canyon,* 73
Oil states, 5, 154–55; Alaska, 10; Gulf coast, 14–18, 30
OPEC, 3, 18, 81–91, 93, 95, 97, 100–3, 108, 130–31
Outer Continental Shelf, 50–56, 66, 68–74, 97, 100, 112, 122–23, 131–32; Gulf of Mexico, 54–55, 94; California